THE GLOBAL FACTORY
Analysis and Action for a New Economic Era

by Rachael Kamel

 American Friends Service Committee

cover photo: Rally in Columbus, Ohio, in support of the Community Readjustment Act, a bill intended to offset the effects of plant closings (1979). **Steve Cagan/Impact Visuals.**

Designed by Rachael Kamel and Gerry Henry.

Printed in the United States of America by Omega Press.

ISBN: 0-910082-15-4

Library of Congress Cataloging-in-Publication Data

Kamel, Rachael
      The global factory : analysis and action for a new economic era / by Rachael Kamel
      vi + 94 pp. 21.5 X 25 cm
      Includes bibliographical references
      ISBN 0-910082-15-4 : $7.50
      1. International business enterprises—Social aspects. 2. International division of labor. 3. Labor movement. I. Title.
HD2755.5.K354 1990   89-18146
338.8—dc20   CIP

Contents

Unemployed groups from across the United States rally at the Capitol to demand jobs in this 1983 demonstration.

JIM WEST/IMPACT VISUALS

Preface

Through its work in the United States and abroad, the American Friends Service Committee (AFSC) has come to recognize that one of the most pervasive forms of violence in the world today is the violence of economic exploitation. We see the lives and futures of families, communities, and whole countries blighted when an unbridled search for profits overrides consideration of the social good.

The AFSC seeks to root out the causes of violence that lie in poverty and imbalance of wealth and to help establish the conditions in which all women and men can live in dignity. This work reflects Friends' view of the sacredness of each human being. Action on this belief has carried the AFSC into programs of service and advocacy, of organizing, education, and development at home and around the world. *The Global Factory* is an outgrowth of several significant strands of that work.

AFSC has worked along the Mexico-U.S. border for more than twenty years on programs dealing with health, human rights, and economic development. In the 1970s we became concerned about the impact of *maquiladoras*, the foreign- (mainly U.S.-) owned assembly plants in Mexico strung along the 2000-mile border between the two countries. We saw at first, most vividly, the impact on the health and safety of the young Mexican women who worked in the plants and the serious distortion of the economic development of the borderlands.

In the context of its Mexico-U.S. Border Program, concerned with the causes and consequences of the movement of peoples to the north and capital to the south across the border, AFSC undertook a Maquila Project. We focused on activities in support of the *maquila* workers as they sought to improve their living and working conditions. Throughout that work, we have gained understanding of the human dimensions of global issues. We are acutely aware of the violence of poverty and exploitation as it is manifested in the lives of women workers and their families. And we are made humble by their steady courage and resilience. We seek to advocate for their concerns within the United States. Most recently we have sought to broaden awareness in the United States of the *maquila* phenomenon and its consequences. This guide is one tool in that effort.

In the course of this work, we have become increasingly aware of the other side of the *maquiladoras*—their harmful impact on the many U.S. workers who are left behind as their jobs move across the border. We began to see the need for a direct dialog between these two groups of workers—both caught in the grips of the same large-scale economic phenomena, both with little information about the lives and aspirations of their counterparts on the other side of the border. Increasingly, our work has reflected this emphasis on cross-border communication.

Maquilas, of course, have their parallels in many nations around the world, in Asia, Latin America and the Caribbean, and, increasingly, Africa. In all of these areas young women have been targeted as a primary labor force for transnational corporations, as manufacturing plants leave the advanced industrial world in search of ever-cheaper labor. The problems associated with this new "global factory"—unjust and inhuman living and working conditions, sexual exploitation, social disruption, and distorted economic development—appear to be virtually universal.

In 1978 the Nationwide Women's Program, another unit of AFSC, publicly launched its project on Women and Global Corporations: Work, Roles, Resistance. This effort continues to promote networking and communication links among the workers, activists, and researchers who are concerned with the global factory as a women's issue. Addressing the needs of women in the transnational workforce, they are finding, requires a new way of looking at labor issues. Especially through the work of Third World women's movements, a new synthesis is emerging of feminist perspectives, trade unionism, and grassroots popular organizing.

Within AFSC, the Maquila Project and the Women and Global Corporations Project have collaborated for many years, each enriching the other in countless ways. *The Global Factory* is the latest such collaboration. It grows out of everything we have learned, through our own work and by listening to the experiences of others, about the negative impact of TNCs on a large majority of the world's peoples.

This guide is based in our perception that more and more people within the United States are seeking a deeper understanding of the international economy, as they identify global economic trends as a major source of their local economic problems. It also represents our conviction that women's stories and women's perspectives must be a central foundation of any attempt to come to terms with the global economy.

The Global Factory appears at a moment of great pain and great promise. Environmental devastation, economic crisis, poverty and social dislocation—all are growing realities in the United States as well as the Third World. By the same token, however, more and more groups are realizing that we must talk with one another and work together in order to bring about positive change. International people-to-people cooperation has become as vital as cooperation across the divisions of class, race, and gender.

It is in that spirit of dialog and cooperation that we offer this guide. Our hope is that it will be a useful tool for the development of powerful coalitions to demand and help fashion a more just and humane economy, in the United States and throughout the world—one in which all people can live in dignity.

—Barbara W. Moffett and Saralee Hamilton

Acknowledgments

From the initial concept through the finished product, many people and organizations have participated in making this book a reality.

Within AFSC, a staff working group oversaw the development and realization of this guide, composed of Saralee Hamilton, coordinator of the Nationwide Women's Program; Betty Baumann, director of the Maquila Project; and Barbara Moffett, secretary of the Community Relations Division, within which work on the border is included. Administrative support and research assistance were provided by Holli Van Nest, with additional administrative support by Sol Maria Rivera. Valuable support and feedback were also provided by members of the Maquila Task Force, an advisory committee for the work of the Maquila Project, including Maya Miller, Stan Bittinger, and Shelley Coppock.

In the project's initial phases, Shelley Coppock worked extensively to develop the concept and format of the guide, and she also contributed the chapter on leading a discussion of global factory issues. Chat Canlas, a former fellow at the Institute for Policy Studies, contributed the chapter on the Philippines. Background materials for the chapter on plant closings were compiled by Anne Lawrence and Jan Gilbrecht, using the files of the Oakland Plant Closures Project. Mary Norris copy-edited the final manuscript.

Many friends and colleagues read the manuscript and offered their comments, including Mark Burnette, Judy Claude, Pat Cooper, Tom Fenton, Joan First, Jane Fleishman, Roberta Foss, Freja Kamel, Jack Metzgar, Joyce Miller, Laurie Nissonoff, Holly Sklar, Ted Smukler, Ellen Tichenor, Leah Wise, and Warren Witte. Alicia Gurdián was an unfailing source of feedback and moral support.

The Center for Popular Economics generously gave permission to copy statistics from their *Field Guide to the U.S. Economy*. The Council on International and Public Affairs also helped with statistics and background information about the U.S. economy. The Media Network made available their database on activist films and videos to assist in preparation of the resource guide in chapter 7.

Grateful acknowledgment is made to all those whose names are listed and to the workers and activists around the world whose courage and wisdom have made this guide possible.

Introduction

We live in an era of tremendous economic change. The types of jobs we do, the settings we work in, what we can look forward to in our future—all have changed dramatically in less than a single generation, and further changes are in store. Businesses are growing larger and larger, and now many corporations span half the globe. Automation and new information technology are making some jobs obsolete, moving others abroad, and changing the very nature of many that remain.

Nearly all of us are affected by these changes. As fewer jobs pay wages that can support a family, more and more women will spend their adult lives in the paid workforce—by choice for some, by necessity for others. Increasing numbers of families are headed by women, whose lower incomes often spell poverty for themselves and their children. Plants that close to move to other regions of the country or overseas can leave entire communities economically devastated. Our society as a whole is growing more economically polarized, with the rich growing richer and the poor growing poorer. At the same time, many more people are falling into poverty. As this polarization worsens, the gap is widening between whites and people of color, especially African-Americans.

Most of us who are working adults today came of age in the post–World War II "American Century," when the U.S. economy became the largest and most powerful economy in the world. The media trumpeted the American Dream of affluence, economic security, and home ownership. For poor people, whether whites or people of color, this never was much more than a dream. Today, even the formerly secure middle class has watched its standard of living erode steadily for the last fifteen years as incomes have failed to keep pace with inflation. Unemployment rates once considered shocking are now defined as normal.

New technology or the "Information Age" is often hyped as the solution to our economic problems. In the "post-industrial" United States, the story goes, we will all be white-collar workers, computer-age professionals who never dirty our hands. But all too often new technology means that a $12-per-hour factory job in the Industrial

How to Use This Guide

This guide is intended as an aid to planning educational and action-oriented programs on the global factory. Depending on your interests, each chapter may be used alone or in combination with other sections. A brief summary of the contents is included here to help you determine which parts of the guide will be most useful to you.

Chapter 1 provides an overview of the global economy, showing how different economic symptoms all spring from the same underlying causes. To illustrate the international dimensions of the problem, chapters 2 to 4 zero in on three different national examples: plant closings in the United States, U.S.-owned factories or *maquiladoras* in Mexico, and labor issues in the Philippines.

Chapter 5 surveys the rich variety of initiatives underway in the United States to link up working people internationally. Chapter 6 offers suggestions on how to get a project started—whether it is a single discussion or class session, an ongoing research/action group, or anything in between. An extensive resource list in chapter 7 suggests audiovisual materials and publications for discussion or further study and gives the addresses of organizations working on related issues. A glossary at the end of the guide defines some terms that may be unfamiliar.

Heartland is transformed into a minimum-wage job in the Southwest—or a job in Mexico paying $3.25 for a day's hard labor. Many women who work behind a computer terminal are finding that high tech means high stress: mindless jobs in which a computer monitors every keystroke, as clerical work is transformed into a new kind of assembly line. Most of the new jobs being created today are low-paying service jobs with few benefits, and more and more people are working full time at jobs that cannot raise their families out of poverty.

Economic hard times bring a host of social problems in their wake. Alcoholism, domestic violence, suicide—all are increased by unemployment and other forms of economic dislocation. Women who work outside the home must still shoulder the lion's share of responsibility for raising children, caring for the sick and elderly, and performing daily household tasks. Thousands of communities are burdened with toxic waste dumps, and the terrible environmental toll of corporate growth is becoming increasingly clear. Racist violence and attacks on gays and lesbians are undergoing a frightening resurgence, as some people direct their anger onto society's traditional scapegoats.

All of the phenomena we have mentioned are interrelated. They are part of the restructuring of individual national economies into an integrated global economy dominated by transnational corporations, which are based mainly in the United States, Japan, and western Europe. Women in the Caribbean island of Barbados do the word processing for corporations headquartered in New York. Workers in Mexico manufacture windshield wipers that used to be made in Buffalo. Malaysian women whose families have been subsistence farmers for centuries now work in huge factories, sewing jeans or assembling consumer electronics for the U.S. market.

For workers in the Third World, the new global economy also poses grim problems. Wages range from just over $2 an hour in Hong Kong or Taiwan to as low as 40 cents an hour in Mexico. Health and safety are often virtually unregulated. Many young women start working as young as sixteen and are unable to continue by the time they are twenty-five because their health is broken. Attempts to organize labor unions are often violently suppressed by government soldiers—soldiers who are frequently armed and trained with U.S. tax dollars. Many Third World nations, especially in Latin America, face a crippling burden of debt to U.S.

banks, so that social resources are used to pay interest rather than to provide services like education or health care.

Yet, in many places, these problems have sparked not passive resignation but a renewed determination on the part of ordinary people to take control of their own lives. In country after country, organizing is on the upswing, mounting a potent challenge to the dominance of U.S.-based corporations and their allies among traditional economic elites.

Here in the United States, the 1980s have meant the erosion or loss of many of the rights and social benefits we have gained since the Great Depression more than fifty years ago. To take just one example, the Reagan Administration's housing policies, which cut funding for low-income housing by 75 percent, are related to the astronomical growth of homelessness. To describe the social, environmental, and civil rights programs that were hamstrung or eliminated in the past decade would fill another book.

Troublesome as these policies may be, it is important to realize that the changes we have described are not the work of any one administration or either political party. This guide is concerned with structural changes in the economy that run far deeper than any change in Washington. The challenge that confronts us is no less than the challenge of standing up to the transnational corporations, forcing them to respond to the human needs of workers, communities, and entire nations. Campaigns for enlightened legislation and regulation are key tools in that task, but they must be complemented by workplace and community organizing around a host of issues.

In hundreds of places across the United States, such organizing is already underway. Where plants have closed down, local coalitions have sprung up to demand corporate accountability and advocate alternatives for blighted communities. Public awareness of the problem of corporate flight is at an all-time high. Other groups focus on health and environmental hazards in the workplace, holding corporations accountable for harming workers and the local environment. Still others seek to build international ties, bringing together workers from many countries who work in the same industry. Others approach international issues by opposing investment in apartheid South Africa or focusing on the role of corporate power in war-torn regions like Central America or the Philippines.

The constituencies for such efforts are many. Trade unions, other types of labor groups, churches and synagogues, community and women's organizations, environmentalists, and groups opposed to U.S. intervention abroad—all have a common interest in restraining corporate power. Internationally, people-to-people communication and cooperation are vital: we need multinational movements to stand up to the transnational corporations. Throughout the Third World, workers pressing for labor rights, communities concerned for economic survival, and all those committed to people-oriented development are actively seeking to build alliances with movements in the industrialized countries.

If we are to achieve our goals, however, all of these efforts must grow—not only in size but also in their capacity to work together. None of these movements, in the United States or internationally, can succeed alone. To be effective, we need to build powerful coalitions that can represent the concerns of all who are negatively affected by the new global economy.

Realizing this vision means that we must take a hard look at inequalities among working people—both within the United States and between the United States and the Third World. Both nationally and internationally, the workforce is stratified by race, gender, and nationality. If we fail to take this reality into account, we may fall into the trap of fighting for the benefit of the more privileged at the expense of the less privileged. If, however, we strive to understand the experience of all sectors of working people, we can find common ground among groups that have seldom believed they have anything in common.

The Global Factory is intended to be a resource for groups and individuals who seek to address these issues and build such coalitions. While this guide tries to convey a sense of certain Third World realities, its focus is on the United States: the problems faced by U.S. working people, their links to the global economy, and the range of organizing strategies that are currently being explored. We have emphasized how U.S. groups inside and outside the labor movement are making links with workers' groups and movements in the Third World.

Standing up to transnational corporations may seem daunting. We often hear of the size and power of these businesses, but seldom receive news of those who have successfully called them to account. Many of us are not accustomed to hearing economic issues explained in plain language, so we believe we cannot understand them. Also, groups in this country often are not used to cooperating with other movements or constituencies, especially across boundaries of race, class, gender, or language.

If the challenges are great, so too are the promises. By working together across borders and other barriers, we can take part in creating the history of our times—into the next century.

THE COSTS OF UNEMPLOYMENT

Each 1% increase in the unemployment rate sustained over a period of six years is associated with:

37,000 total deaths
920 suicides
650 homicides
500 deaths from cirrhosis of the liver
4000 state mental hospital admissions
3300 state prison admissions

Source: The Deindustrialization of America

1. Overview: The U.S. Economy Goes Global

In today's economy, imports are everywhere. A majority of the clothing sold in the United States bears a label saying it was made in another country. The same is true of many consumer electronic goods, such as televisions or personal computers.

Usually, imports made in places like Japan, such as VCRs or automobiles, receive the most media attention. But in many cases products with U.S. brand names are also manufactured abroad, by U.S. firms that have moved their production operations out of the country.

These imports are only one manifestation of a phenomenon that has changed the face of the world economy: the growth of many large corporations into giants operating around the globe. These transnational corporations (TNCs) are generally based in the United States, western Europe, or Japan. Today, they dominate the world economic scene, with annual sales that outstrip the budgets of many nations. Banks, agribusiness, manufacturing firms, and now service industries are increasingly in the hands of global corporations.

TNCs are not a new invention by any means. They have been growing in number and size since the end of World War II, and their roots are far older. In manufacturing, different countries have been assigned different—and unequal—roles in production for centuries. Throughout the era of colonialism, European powers and later the United States extracted raw materials from Third World nations for processing into manufactured goods. We could even date the beginnings of the global economy back to the 1500s, when European adventurers came to the New World to plunder Indian gold.

What is new is the *global factory*, in which a single manufacturing process is broken down into many steps that are divided among workers in different nations (or different areas of a single country). Management control, as well as research and development and product design, stays in the hands of the parent firm in the United States (or another advanced industrial country). Meanwhile, fabrication of components or final assembly is carried out in Third World countries like Korea, the Philippines, or Mexico—or in a low-wage area of the United States.

Whether the product is clothing that is cut in the United States and sewn in Ciudad Juarez, or computer chips that are designed and printed in California and cut and bonded in Malaysia, the process is similar. This way of organizing production is a new historical development, dating back hardly more than twenty years. Most important, it underlies many of the plant shutdowns and lost jobs that have ravaged the U.S. economy throughout that period.

This chapter offers an overview of the global factory, describing where it came

New York City, 1989: Teenage worker in a garment sweatshop.

from and how it works. It explores the impact of this new system on ordinary working people and their communities, in the United States and the Third World. The chapter closes with a look at some larger implications of these economic trends.

LEAVING THE UNITED STATES

Why did the global factory develop?

Corporations have always searched for ways to boost profits by lowering labor costs. This may involve automation—using increased investment in machinery to reduce reliance on human labor. Or it may mean increasing the productivity of workers, through technological innovations or speed-ups.

Some industrial processes are more labor-intensive—they do not lend themselves easily to automation. Wages and benefits thus make up a large percentage of total production costs. In such cases, the drive to lower costs often takes the form of the "runaway shop," or relocation to an area where workers will accept lower pay and harsher working conditions. In earlier generations, for example, the U.S. textile industry abandoned large numbers of mills in the heavily unionized Northeast to move to the South, where living standards were lower, land and water were cheaper, and workers faced greater obstacles in organizing labor unions.

The United States emerged from World War II with the strongest economy in the world—in large part because its cities and factories sustained no wartime damage. By the 1960s and 1970s, U.S. manufacturers were facing increasing competition from the rebuilt economies of Europe and Japan. To maintain their market position, U.S. firms needed to cut costs.

Before the mid-1960s, the costs of transportation and delays in communication deterred most U.S. firms from manufacturing overseas. It was too difficult to control quality or adjust production processes to quickly changing markets.

Since then, new developments in communications technology have made it possible to harmonize different stages of production in separate parts of the world. Computers and satellites permit instantaneous transmission of data, so production remains a single integrated process. Also, container ships and air travel have made the transportation of components and finished products significantly faster.

Thus, through the computer revolution, labor-intensive industries have been able to expand their constant search for lower costs into all areas of the world. Now they can take advantage of labor markets in Third World countries where workers earn as little as 40 cents an hour.

Electronics assembly and the "fiber industries"—garments and textiles—are the best-known examples of industries involved in the global factory. Other labor-intensive industries that have been affected include footwear, knitwear, leather products, electrical products, optical goods, plastics, toys, and sporting goods.

A more recent trend is for heavy industry to join the exodus from the United States. On the Mexico-U.S. border, for example, the fastest-growing sector is the automotive industry. Steel, machine tools, airplanes, construction equipment, and tractors also are moving abroad. The global factory has advanced to a stage in which it involves the entire U.S. industrial base.

The newest trend is for service industries to transfer operations to the Third World. In some Caribbean countries, for instance, women perform data entry operations in factory-style settings, linked by satellite to huge banks or insurance firms in the United States.

What is the impact of the global factory on the U.S. economy?

U.S.-owned corporations represent about half of the 500 largest corporations in the world. According to figures gathered by the United Electrical Workers union (UE), these U.S.-based TNCs have more than 18,000 subsidiaries in foreign countries and employ almost seven million foreign workers. In comparison, some nineteen million U.S. workers are employed in manufacturing.

When U.S.-owned corporations produce goods in other countries, the value of those goods, as well as the jobs of the workers who produced them, are lost to the U.S. economy. In 1985, foreign factories owned by U.S. corporations produced goods worth $294 billion—more than the value of all U.S. exports for that year. About $37 billion

FALLING PROFITS SPUR THE GLOBAL FACTORY

The real rate of return (after-tax profits, adjusted for inflation) for U.S. nonfinancial corporations fell from the mid-1960s until the recession of 1981-82. Since then, spurred by corporate tax cuts, plant closings, and wage reductions, profits have been rising again.

Overall profit rates were:

15.5% for 1963-66
12.7% for 1967-70
10.1% for 1971-74
9.7% for 1975-78
4.5% for 1980
7.0% for 1984
7.2% for 1986

Source: The Deindustrialization of America; The Great U-Turn

worth was sold in the domestic U.S. market—20 percent of all goods imported in that year.

For many people, the increasing availability of imported goods in the U.S. market is an emblem of U.S. economic decline. The trade deficit—caused when U.S. corporations import more than they export—has received enormous media attention over the past few years, probably more than any other issue in the U.S. economy. Discussions of the trade deficit almost always focus on ''foreign competition'' as the key problem. However, U.S.-owned firms still account for the same share of world exports as they did thirty years ago—about 18 percent. The only thing that has changed is that today their products are being exported from somewhere else.

How are ordinary working people affected in the United States?

The global factory is one cause of the ''deindustrialization'' of the United States. Manufacturing jobs are on the decline, while most new jobs are in the lower-paying service sector. This means that often people who lose their jobs because a plant closes down cannot find a new job at the same wages. Studies of displaced workers have found people forced to take new jobs with wage cuts ranging from 12 to 40 percent.

For corporations, moving may be an attractive way to boost profits. For workers and their communities, however, the consequences are often grim. Workers faced with plant shutdowns lose much more than wages and benefits. They may lose their homes, their cars, and their savings. They may also lose their sense of themselves as productive workers and providers for their family. The security of people's future, their dignity, and their sense of control over their lives are at risk. The stress related to job loss has been shown to result in increased rates of suicide, homicide, heart disease, alcoholism, mental illness, domestic violence, and family breakup.

When a company closes down, an entire community may be hit with a large problem. Generally, for each manufacturing job that is lost, three-and-a-half additional jobs are affected—in support industries, service industries, and local small businesses. As jobs are lost, local governments face a drop in income from both corporate taxes and local taxes paid by employees. At the same time, the demand for social services goes up, as newly unemployed members of the community try to adjust.

The issue of plant closures is explored in more detail in chapter 2.

How does the global factory affect men and women differently in the United States?

When we imagine who is affected by plant closings, the typical image that comes to mind is a male worker in a heavy industry like steel or automobiles. Women are not seen as part of the picture, except perhaps as the wives of laid-off workers.

In fact, though, women are at least 35 percent of the workers displaced by plant closings, according to a study by the federal Bureau of Labor Statistics (BLS) that covered the years from 1979 to 1983. This study did not even count many displaced women workers, because it did not consider small shops of less than 100 workers, which are far more likely to employ women.

When displaced workers find new jobs, both men and women suffer heavy wage cuts. Because women earn less to begin with, however, their wage losses may take them down well below the poverty level.

Women and men are employed differently in manufacturing, so they are often affected differently by large-scale economic trends. Women workers are heavily concentrated in labor-intensive manufacturing, especially the fiber industries. Male workers are concentrated in capital-intensive industries like autos or steel—those where capital goods (machinery) represent a greater proportion of the costs of production.

Industries with a predominantly female workforce are often seen as marginal to the economy. However, the fiber industries still employ more workers than basic steel, auto assembly, and chemical refining combined. And this is true even though the fiber industries have lost some 800,000 jobs over the past twenty years.

Labor-intensive industries with a predominantly female workforce—garment and textiles, electrical and electronics assembly, and others—were the first to be drawn into the global factory. They have been moving abroad for more than twenty years. The international movement of capital-intensive industries is a much more recent phenomenon and was not common before the 1970s.

Just in the past two or three years, the global factory has become a more public issue in the United States. As more U.S. jobs move to Mexico and other Third World countries, large labor unions, members of

CHANGING FAMILY COMPOSITION

Today, only a minority of U.S. families include a married couple and their children. One of the biggest changes is in the number of people living by themselves. Between 1950 and 1986, single-person households increased from 9% to 23% of all U.S. households. Another key change has been in the number of women-headed households. When families with children that are maintained by women are counted as a percentage of all families with children under age 18, their numbers have risen rapidly:

**7% in 1960
10% in 1970
19% in 1985**

Source: Center for Popular Economics

Congress, and other public figures are speaking out. The media are also beginning to take notice in new ways. Some feminists have noted that as long as the global factory affected mainly women's jobs, it was essentially invisible. Today, when men's jobs are increasingly affected, the global factory is more widely recognized as a serious problem for U.S. workers.

In part, this is because women tend to work in much smaller shops—a characteristic of labor-intensive industries. When a garment shop with twenty or fifty employees closes down, the closure is far less noticeable than the loss of an automotive plant with 1000 workers or more.

Another factor is certainly the persistent idea that women's work is simply not as important as men's. And, when women are invisible, their needs are not fully taken into account in public policy debates.

In fact, women's jobs are clearly crucial to the security and survival of themselves and their families. One study of married women with factory jobs found them contributing 45 percent of their family's income. Also, as family living patterns change, more and more women are supporting a household on their income alone.

Generally, the jobs women do in manufacturing are more likely to be defined as "unskilled" and to pay much lower wages than men's jobs. Yet factory jobs still pay substantially more than other jobs available to women, like waitressing or clerical work. For generations, immigrant women and women of color in particular have relied on factory work as a way to achieve a minimal level of economic stability. As manufacturing is restructured—through the global factory and other related trends—this option is rapidly being foreclosed.

What is the attitude of the U.S. government toward the global factory?

From the beginning, the economic policies of the U.S. government have promoted the movement of jobs out of the country. In the mid-1960s, articles 806 and 807 of the U.S. Tariff Schedule (see box on page 8) were changed to reduce greatly the import duties on U.S. goods that are shipped abroad for assembly and then reimported into the U.S. for sale.

In 1976, the Generalized System of Preferences (GSP) was established to permit duty-

JUDY JANDA/IMPACT VISUALS

free imports of certain products from developing countries into the United States. Likewise, since 1984 the Caribbean Basin Initiative (CBI) has allowed imports to enter duty-free from selected nations in Central America and the Caribbean. Although the GSP and CBI are supposedly intended to promote economic development in the Third World, in fact the benefits of these schemes are reaped by U.S.-based TNCs that set up shop abroad.

U.S. government policies benefit the transnationals in additional ways. Corporations that pay taxes to foreign governments receive a tax credit in the United States. Note that this is not a tax *deduction* (which would mean that income paid out as taxes to other governments would not be taxed in the United States), but a dollar-for-dollar *credit*— every dollar paid out to a foreign government is subtracted from the firm's U.S. taxes.

U.S.-owned corporations are insured against both natural and political disasters by another government program—the Overseas Private Investment Corporation (OPIC). Under this system, if a TNC is affected by political turmoil or civil war in the Third World, its losses are made up by U.S. taxpayers. Other incentives are noted in the box below.

The United States also plays a dominant role in two key international institutions of the global factory—the World Bank and the International Monetary Fund (IMF). These two agencies, which control loans and credit to Third World governments, effectively dictate the types of development policies these governments may pursue. They bear a large share of the responsibility for the prominence of export-oriented development schemes that are geared to the needs of TNCs, not local populations. And, as described below in the discussion of the international debt crisis, the IMF also intervenes in the domestic economic policies of many Third World governments, demanding harsh "austerity" plans in return for continuing credit.

ECONOMIC CONCENTRATION

The largest corporations continue to absorb a greater and greater share of total assets in the U.S. economy. The percent of total assets of nonfinancial corporations held by the top 100 industrial firms was:

44% in 1961
51% in 1970
61% in 1984

Source: Center for Popular Economics

U.S. Government Policy Promotes The Global Factory

Articles 806/807, U.S. Tariff Schedule—Article 807 applies to goods fabricated from U.S. components that are sent abroad for assembly. When the finished product is reimported into the U.S. for sale, a tariff is assessed only on the "value added" during assembly—that is, the cost of the labor involved. Article 806 provides that metal products may be exported from the United States for processing (bending, punching, drilling, etc.), provided that at least one further processing step occurs when the item is returned to the United States. Again, duty is paid only on the value added. In practice, Article 807 accounts for more than 98 percent of the manufacturing that takes place under these two programs. An amended provision known as "Super 807" provides even greater incentives to garment manufacturers to move abroad.

Generalized System of Preferences (GSP)—Established in 1976, the GSP permits designated developing countries to obtain duty-free access to the U.S. market for many items. For goods to qualify, 35 percent of their entering value must be produced in one or more of the countries named as beneficiaries of the program. The products included are named each year by the U.S. president. Limitations are set for the total dollar volume and percentage of total U.S. imports for each item. In general, products covered by import quotas, such as garments or leather goods, are not included in the GSP. In 1984, the GSP was modified to limit participation by the most heavily industrialized Third World countries, such as Hong Kong, Korea, or Mexico.

Caribbean Basin Initiative (CBI)—Since 1984, Caribbean and Central American nations have been eligible to participate in this program, which offers duty-free access to U.S. markets for twelve years. Twenty countries have joined the program. The rules are similar to those for the GSP: at least 35 percent of the value of the products entering the U.S. must originate in beneficiary nations. Excluded are goods covered by quotas, such as garments and leather goods, petroleum and petroleum products, and canned tuna fish. Almost all other products can enter duty-free.

Tax incentives—Corporations that pay income taxes to foreign governments can take a tax credit that permits them to subtract an equivalent amount from their U.S. corporate income taxes. In addition, corporations can defer payment of U.S. income taxes on overseas profits until the profits enter the United States. This creates an incentive for companies to shift operations abroad and reinvest their profits in foreign operations.

Semiconductors—Since 1985, certain semiconductors have been permitted to enter the United States duty-free from all countries that have the trade status of Most Favored Nation. This includes advanced industrial countries such as Canada, Japan, and France, as well as many developing countries.

Sources: Journal of the Flagstaff Institute' X:2' 1986' and United Electrical Workers.

MOVING TO THE THIRD WORLD

Why has the global factory moved production to the Third World?

For the Third World, the global factory is only the newest development in a long history of foreign domination.

Third World countries are the former colonies of western Europe and the United States in Africa, Asia, and Latin America. Some—especially in Latin America—achieved political independence as early as the mid-1800s. Others—like the southern African nations of Angola and Mozambique—became self-governing as late as 1975. But most became independent nations in the years after World War II.

A few countries are still ruled as "possessions" of the United States or a European power. A key example is Puerto Rico, which is considered by the United Nations to be a separate country governed as a U.S. colony but is claimed by the United States as a "commonwealth."

In many countries, political independence has not been followed by economic independence. The colonial governments are gone, but transnational corporations continue to dominate the country's economic life. Local elites often set priorities for development that do not meet the needs of their own people. In many countries, the economic interests of traditional elites are tied to the TNCs in a host of ways, direct and indirect. Such elite groups often pursue policies that enrich themselves and favor the TNCs—at their countries' expense.

Distorted development means that most people in the Third World continue to live in bitter poverty, although their countries may be rich in natural resources and fertile land. Unemployment and underemployment are widespread. Because so many people are desperate and have few alternatives, they are seen by TNCs as an ideal pool of cheap labor. Typical hourly wages paid by TNCs in the Third World range from a high of $2.12 in Taiwan down to 40 cents in Mexico.

There are many differences among Third World countries, including how they are involved in the global factory. This chapter offers a general picture of some overall characteristics. Chapters 3 and 4 take a closer look at two specific examples—Mexico and the Philippines.

How is the global factory organized in Third World countries?

TNCs operate in Third World economies in a variety of ways. Our focus in this guide is on manufacturing plants in special areas known as *export processing zones* (EPZs) or free trade zones. Inside these huge industrial parks, host governments offer a variety of concessions to attract foreign investment. These concessions are justified by arguments

Maquila workers neighborhood in Matamoros, Mexico, just across the border from Brownsville, Texas. Living conditions like these are typical for TNC workers in many countries.

PEGGY FOGARTY/AFSC

MANUFACTURING WORLDWIDE

Below are average manufacturing wages for 1987, in dollars per hour:

Mexico—$0.97
Brazil—$1.10
South Korea—$1.43
Hong Kong—$2.04
Taiwan—$2.12
Japan—$9.92
Sweden—$10.57
United States—$10.82
W. Germany—$13.16

Source: Labor Research Review

that the TNCs will create jobs and provide a source of foreign exchange, both of which are sorely needed in many Third World countries.

TNCs are given special exemptions from the host countries' usual import and export tariffs, allowing duty-free access to raw materials, components, and capital equipment. Often the TNCs are provided with infrastructural support, including subsidized gas and the rental of factory buildings. Some countries offer financial incentives, including financing and low-interest loans. TNCs may also benefit from "tax holidays" of five to fifteen years, during which they do not have to pay corporate income taxes to local governments. Environmental regulations are often relaxed or ignored to benefit the TNCs.

In addition, labor rights are often restricted or eliminated inside the export processing zones. In many countries, strikes have been declared illegal and violently suppressed by police or military forces.

By the mid-1980s, there were seventy-nine of these special economic zones, operating in thirty-five different countries. U.S. companies have set up plants in Central America, including El Salvador, Honduras, and Guatemala; in the Caribbean, including Haiti, Puerto Rico, Jamaica, and the Dominican Republic; and in Asia, including Taiwan, Korea, Malaysia, Singapore, and Thailand.

What are working conditions like in the export processing zones?

TNCs try to boost their profit margin in many ways, not only by paying lower wages. Production is often speeded up from U.S. standards by 25 percent or more when a plant moves abroad, while working hours are increased by an average of 50 percent. About 85 percent of the workers in EPZs are young women, who may start working at sixteen years of age. By the time they are twenty-five, many are unable to continue working at that pace, and so they must try to find other work.

Women in nearly every country report that sexual harassment is a serious problem in export processing plants. Supervisors are nearly always men, and often they demand sexual services in exchange for a good rating. Asian women have named this the "lay down or be laid off" policy.

Health and safety is another major issue for EPZ workers. Women in many countries work with toxic chemicals without warnings or safety equipment. Electronics workers

peer through a microscope all day to inspect silicon chips. After a few years, their vision may be permanently blurred, and they too must look for another job.

From the point of view of the TNCs, the lack of regulations governing workplace health and safety is another opportunity to boost profits by lowering costs. The same holds true of environmental restrictions, which are lax or nonexistent in most Third World countries. Meanwhile, entire communities are placed at risk by toxic exposure.

A crucial feature of the global factory is that transnational plants are highly mobile, moving from country to country within the Third World. Thus, TNCs can pressure both workers and governments for greater concessions—because the threat of relocation and mass layoffs is always present. After more than a decade of organizing, labor activists in Asia have learned a lot about dealing with TNCs. Now, they say, many plants are moving on to African countries, where the global factory is unfamiliar and local governments have little knowledge of the health and environmental threats involved.

Why are there so many people available to work in export processing zones?

Traditionally, a large majority of people in Third World countries have been peasants engaged in subsistence agriculture. In recent decades, however, vast sections of land in many countries have been taken over by transnational agribusiness firms. Land is devoted to producing cash crops for export, rather than food for local consumption. Peasant families either lose their land outright or find that they cannot survive economically by farming their own land.

In the search for jobs, entire families may migrate to urban areas. Or a family may send one or more members to the city to seek employment. These members send home cash to help the family survive on the land. Often the older daughters in a family are the ones who work in EPZs.

In many countries, however, the jobs are not there to meet the needs of these displaced populations. Thus, many Third World governments welcome foreign investment as a source of jobs that local economies cannot supply.

In the 1980s, an international debt crisis has dramatically worsened the problems of unemployment and economic dislocation in many Third World countries. For TNCs, this means that the available labor force is even larger. More detail on the debt crisis is provided later in this chapter.

If young women are pushed into industrial employment by economic need, they are also pulled by the hope of a better life. For many women, factory work is a step up. In Mexico, for example, the most common form of paid employment for women is domestic service—which is isolating, pays next to nothing for extremely long hours, and leaves women highly vulnerable to sexual exploitation by their employers.

In contrast, a factory job may offer women a chance for greater personal independence, as well as increases in income and consumption levels. Women's stories collected in the Philippines reveal that many women hope they will be able to continue their education while they work. Studies from various countries (including the United States) have shown that women generally feel they benefit from paid work. In many cases, their desire is not to return to more traditional roles but to win fair wages and working conditions.

AMY ZIMMERMAN/IMPACT VISUALS

Maquila workers labor nine-and-a-half hours a day for 55 cents an hour to make automatic garage door parts for Sears at this plant in Nogales, Sonora, across the border from Nogales, Arizona.

Why do the TNCs hire mainly women?

Women are preferred as employees primarily because they can be paid even less than men. Women's work is undervalued in other countries, just as it is in the United States. The wages of women working in export processing plants are in general 20 to 50 percent lower than what men earn in comparable jobs.

A complicated corporate mythology has evolved to justify women's lower status in the labor market. In this view, women are secondary workers, whose commitment to the labor force is disrupted by marriage and childbearing. Women are seen as mainly interested in their homes and families; they work in paid jobs only to supplement a man's earnings.

As in the United States, these rationalizations do not stand up under closer examination. In the Third World, because of the lack of job opportunities for men, women—whether wives or daughters—are often the primary family member bringing money into a household. Further, increasing numbers of women are single heads of households—another parallel to the United States.

Another important part of the corporate rationale is the idea that women are "naturally" docile. As the story goes, they are better able than men to tolerate the monotony of assembly work. Likewise, they are seen as less likely than men to rebel and form labor unions.

Feminist thinkers have argued that all these traits are simply evidence of women's subordination. If women seem docile, it is because of the weight of tradition demanding that they behave deferentially toward men. Docility is a pose, demanded by society and dropped when women are among themselves.

As evidence for this view, researchers Diane Elson and Ruth Pearson cite the case of certain electronics plants on the Mexico-U.S. border. In these plants, a few male workers were added to all-women production lines in the belief that the presence of men would improve the women's work discipline—that is, encourage them to act more submissive. "It is interesting," say Elson and Pearson, "that governments and companies are unwilling to trust completely the . . . docility of women workers and feel a need to reinforce it with [the] suspension of a wide variety of workers' rights." Rather than women being "naturally" docile, they argue, TNCs are simply taking advantage of women's general subordination in society.

Women are also seen as innately suited for the intricate coordination necessary for testing a printed circuit or sewing a garment. Other feminists have noted the contradiction between this idea and the idea that women are only suited for unskilled work. In many cultures, traditional women's tasks such as sewing or embroidery develop their manual dexterity, so they come to factory work already possessing important skills. Because they are learned in the home, however, these abilities remain invisible and unrecognized. A number of researchers have argued that women's jobs are routinely defined as unskilled—and thus paid at a lower rate—regardless of the actual skills involved.

Does the global factory contribute to economic development?

TNCs are often defended on the basis that they bring modernization and industrial development to the Third World, and there is some truth in this view. The TNCs do create large numbers of jobs, and they bring new technology to their host countries. In addition, they bring dollars or other foreign currencies into a country's economy, giving the host government foreign exchange that can be used for purchasing imports or repaying debts to foreign banks.

A wooden platform has been built in this South Korean sweatshop to increase the number of people who can work in the same room.

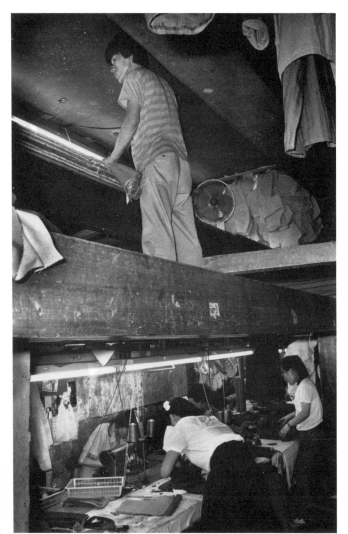

EARL DOTTER

Critics argue, however, that such development serves the needs of the TNCs, not the local population. Jobs in the EPZs are almost invariably extremely low-paying and subject workers to stressful and hazardous conditions. Further, for the vast majority of EPZ workers, the possibilities for occupational advancement are almost nonexistent. Production workers are nearly always women, while all but the lowest level of supervisors are men. It is almost unheard of for women line workers to be trained for technical or management positions. TNCs also do not really contribute to raising the overall technological level of the host country, because the jobs they offer are less-skilled assembly jobs. The global factory is purposely organized so that most jobs are "de-skilled"—workers perform a few simple, repetitive operations without ever learning to understand the technology they are using. Advanced technology may be used, but it is not under local control and it is not transferred to local industry.

Likewise, the inputs for TNC production are mostly imported, processed, and then exported. Because they do not buy components from local producers, TNCs do not stimulate the growth of local industry. And because they are producing for export, they do not contribute to the growth of a local market. TNCs give little back to their host countries in exchange for the concessions they receive. Because they operate in so many countries, they can transfer assets from one branch to another at will. On paper, any given subsidiary may be operating at a loss, and thus pay no taxes to the host government.

A few countries, like Hong Kong, Korea, Taiwan, and Singapore, have been able to build up their own industry while producing for the global economy. In some cases, this is because they pursue more nationalistic policies, such as requiring TNCs to buy a certain percentage of local components. Even so, the wealth that is generated is not shared fairly with the workers who create it, and poverty is still rampant.

In other Third World countries, wealth is simply extracted by foreign corporations and is only shared locally with a tiny elite. The contrasts that are created are extreme. Women work in state-of-the-art high-tech plants, but live in crowded dormitories where they sleep in shifts, three workers sharing a single bed. Governments build modern industrial parks for foreign corporations, while nearby communities go without running water or paved streets.

Is the global factory a modern version of the Industrial Revolution?

Conditions in Third World factories are sometimes compared to those in the Industrial Revolution of the eighteenth and nineteenth centuries, when industry first emerged in the United States, Britain, and other western European countries. Low wages and harsh working conditions in the Third World are similar to those in the early days of manufacturing. Historical accounts tell of children as young as six working ten- and twelve-hour days, chained to their looms, in early textile plants.

It is sometimes argued that wages and working conditions will naturally improve over time in the Third World just as they did in the advanced industrial countries. There are three major problems with this analogy.

First, transnational factories in the Third World are not an independent development, but a subordinate part of a global economic system. Second, with living standards in industrial countries falling steadily, the assumption that conditions will improve as time goes by must be called into question.

Third, and most troubling, affluence in the United States and other advanced industrial countries has always depended on unequal relations with the Third World. From centuries ago, when Africans were kidnapped to provide slave labor for U.S. plantations, to the present-day realities of the global factory, exploitation has been the rule in the international economy.

During the 1980s, the global factory has grown rapidly, while the extremes of poverty in the Third World have also worsened dramatically. Both of these developments are related to the debt crisis.

What is the debt crisis and how is it related to the global factory?

In 1982, the government of Mexico announced that it was unable to meet the interest payments on its multi-billion-dollar foreign debt. The Third World debt crisis, which had been simmering for years, was suddenly front-page news. If Mexico and other developing countries did not continue making payments, it would mean devastating losses for the huge transnational banks, many of which are headquartered in the United States. And if these banks were to be forced into bankruptcy, it would mean the collapse of the entire international financial system.

So far, no debtor country has defaulted outright. To protect their investments, banks and international lending institutions have rescheduled loan repayments and extended additional credit. Meanwhile, throughout the Third World, dozens of countries face crippling burdens of debt to foreign banks, with no solution in sight. National budgets are dominated by debt payments, while schools and clinics are shut down, food subsidies are cut, and development projects come to a halt.

Third World debt has taken its toll on the U.S. economy, too. When other countries' foreign exchange is devoted to debt payments, it cannot be used to purchase imported goods. In 1986, one out of every eight manufacturing jobs in the United States depended on exports. According to one recent estimate, the decline in exports due to the debt crisis has cost the U.S. economy a million jobs.

The U.S. farm crisis has also been deepened by the decline in export markets. For example, in 1981, Latin American nations imported $6.9 billion of U.S. agricultural products, or 15 percent of total U.S. farm exports. By 1985, that figure had fallen to $4.5 billion—a 35-percent drop.

One sector in the United States that has benefited from this situation is the transnational money-center banks, like Chase Manhattan or Citicorp. Their profitability has actually increased as a result of the crisis. At Chase Manhattan, for example, after-tax profits rose from $307 million in 1982 to $565 million in 1985—an increase of almost 46 percent.

The origins of the debt crisis lie in the mid-1970s, when sharply higher oil prices created a large surplus of dollars for oil-exporting nations belonging to the OPEC cartel. These "petrodollars," as they were called, were deposited in large transnational banks. The banks, looking for new opportunities to lend this money out, aggressively promoted massive development projects and arms sales throughout the Third World. The total indebtedness of Third World countries rose from $18 billion in 1971 to $810 billion in 1983.

Several factors have combined to make these debts impossible to repay. Many of the projects they financed were ill-conceived and riddled with corruption. More serious has been the collapse in world commodity prices mentioned above. Prices for oil, raw materials, and agricultural products are now at their lowest levels since the Great Depression of the 1930s. This has caused a major

THE DEBT WAR

"I will tell you that the Third World War has already started— a silent war, not for that reason any the less sinister. This war is tearing down practically all the Third World. Instead of soldiers dying, there are children; instead of millions of wounded, there are millions of unemployed; instead of the destruction of bridges, there is the tearing down of factories, schools, hospitals, and entire economies."

—"Lula" (Luis Ignacio Silva), Brazilian labor leader

The cost of distorted development: unable to gain access to paid employment, squatters in the Philippines scavenge in a garbage dump.

drop in the amount of foreign exchange that Third World countries can earn.

In some countries (examples include Haiti, Nicaragua, and the Philippines), former dictators who saw that their regimes were falling stole vast amounts from their countries' treasuries. Finally, in 1979, as a result of U.S. government monetary policy, interest rates soared around the world. Payments rose steeply at the same time that available funds bottomed out.

The debt crisis has a direct impact on the global factory. To continue receiving credit and avoid default, Third World governments must agree to "austerity programs" demanded by the International Monetary Fund. These programs typically require governments to devalue their currency, cut imports and increase exports, and make deep cuts in social programs.

Devaluation means that a TNC's dollars will buy a lot more in local currency. Devaluation also devastates local economies, so far more workers are unemployed and the bargaining power of labor is reduced. The drive to increase exports means that governments are more eager than ever to court foreign investment. From the point of view of the local governments, the jobs created by TNCs also help to preserve political stability by providing a relief valve for popular discontent. With respect to both workers and local governments, then, the TNCs are in a stronger position than ever.

Meanwhile, vast sums continue to be transferred from the Third World to U.S. and other transnational banks. Between 1982 and 1987, poor countries transferred $140 billion in interest payments to banks in rich countries. This is twice the amount of

reconstruction aid the U.S. sent to Europe after World War II under the Marshall Plan. Some Third World critics charge that the debt has actually been repaid many times, and that only the manipulation of interest rates permits transnational banks to claim they are still owed more.

Because Third World governments are making only interest payments, the amount of principal is never reduced. In recent years, the banks have lent more money to governments to help them make payments on their previous loans. In other words, the banks are now paying themselves, while the amount of debt is growing. By 1987, foreign debt in the Third World topped a trillion dollars.

How is the global factory related to militarism and the threat of war?

Many of the countries with export processing plants are tied militarily to the United States, hosting U.S. bases and receiving millions in U.S. military aid. Often, the governments of these countries receive overt and covert U.S. assistance in maintaining control over their own population.

Around the world, the United States maintains a network of 375 major military bases and hundreds of minor installations. Critics of U.S. foreign policy often charge that this military presence is mainly intended to preserve a climate favorable to U.S.-based transnational corporations. They point to times that the CIA has engineered the overthrow of moderate elected governments that adopted policies opposed by TNCs, including Iran in 1953, Guatemala in 1954, and Chile in 1973. Another example is the U.S. invasion of the Dominican Republic in 1965. Dozens of other examples of such intervention have been documented.

Such U.S. involvement is usually justified as necessary to contain "communist subversion" or "the Soviet threat." But the targets of U.S. intervention are more likely to be land-reform programs or attempts to nationalize industry or natural resources—that is, to reduce or eliminate TNC control of a country's economy.

The stability of the present global economy is seriously threatened by the Third World economic crisis. As human suffering deepens, the demands for a basic change grow louder. Many Third World governments are caught between a rock and a hard place. The reforms demanded by their people and the policies demanded by the TNCs are in direct conflict.

In country after country, governments are responding to cries for reform with repression and massive violations of human rights. When reform is impossible, many people in the Third World see revolution as their only option. As revolutionary pressures mount, the United States responds with ugly wars of counterinsurgency in more and more countries. Each of these wars imposes a bitter cost in death and destruction. And many of them could be the trigger for a nuclear conflict.

The contradiction between human needs and the drive to maximize corporate profits has never been more stark. The economic crisis in the Third World receives little attention in the United States. But it is leading us increasingly to a world where endless war is the norm and nuclear holocaust is a growing possibility.

LOOKING TOWARDS THE FUTURE

What does the global factory mean for our future in the United States?

The decline in manufacturing jobs in the U.S. economy is proceeding quickly and is expected to continue. At present, manufacturing employs 10 to 14 percent of the U.S. workforce; by the year 2005, that figure is expected to shrink to between 2.5 and 5 percent.

Some analysts say that this development is no cause for alarm—that it is part of the natural evolution of the United States into a "postindustrial" society. In this view, high technology holds out the promise of a new economic base that will increase prosperity for U.S. working people. Financial services, computers, research and development, and skilled technical jobs will drive this new information-based economy. Manufacturing will be transferred to countries that are less technologically advanced.

This vision may hold true for engineers, computer professionals, or people with managerial jobs in banking and finance. For the vast majority of the workforce, however, service jobs pay far lower wages. They are much less likely to be unionized or to offer fringe benefits.

For example, half of the new jobs created since 1980 paid wages below the poverty level, according to a report released by the Senate Budget Committee in September 1988. This official poverty line is set at $11,611 for a family of four. More than a third (34.2 percent) of U.S. workers now earn less than that amount, up from 32.4 percent in 1979.

The Senate study found that the proportion of high-paying jobs also increased slightly, from 3.7 to 4.5 percent of the workforce. (High-paying jobs are defined as those paying more than $46,444 a year.)

The loss came in the middle, where the share of the workforce declined from 64 to 61.3 percent of jobs.

The Senate study is one of many indicating that the trend in the United States is toward increasing economic polarization. Rich people are increasing their share of the nation's income, and a small number of professionals are moving upward as the highly visible "yuppies." For much larger numbers of working people, however, times are growing harder as middle-level jobs shrink in number.

Income—and with it, living standards—in the United States has been falling for more than fifteen years. Between 1979 and 1985 alone, real wages (income corrected for inflation) declined by 6 percent. Since 1973, real wages have fallen by 15 percent. For many working people, the prospect of steady employment, a decent income, and a secure future is a vanishing promise. For marginalized groups like people of color or new immigrants, the American Dream is over before it ever began.

Why is manufacturing particularly affected?

Traditionally, manufacturing has been the most heavily unionized sector of the U.S. workforce. Unions have brought higher wages and increased fringe benefits. They have protected workers against arbitrary treatment by bargaining for seniority rights, promotions, and grievance procedures. They have also given workers a voice in demanding safe and healthy working conditions.

When there is a strong union sector, the benefits spill over even to nonunion sectors of the workforce. Other employers pay higher wages to reduce the incentive for their employees to unionize. In addition, over the

THE WIDENING INCOME GAP

In the seven years between 1979 and 1986, although the U.S. economy was expanding steadily, the gap between rich and poor widened considerably. For the poorest fifth of the population, average income (in constant 1986 dollars) fell from $10,246 to $9133, a drop of 10.9%. The top fifth, on the other hand, gained a whopping 13.8%, with average income climbing from $82,666 to $94,104.

Source: Economic Policy Institute

past fifty years the labor movement has won legislation protecting the rights of all workers through Social Security, minimum wage and overtime requirements, unemployment insurance, and workers' compensation.

More recently, other social movements have won prohibitions against age, sex, and race discrimination at work. Affirmative action programs have been instituted in some workplaces. Protections have been established for occupational health and safety. At the same time, restrictions have been placed on environmental pollution, most of which is caused by industry.

All of these gains add to the cost of production in the United States. Another way of saying the same thing is that they force corporations to share a larger percentage of their income with workers and with society as a whole. The amount of income that remains as profit is thus reduced.

From this perspective, the global factory is a strategy to shift the balance of power between labor and capital. The international flight of jobs can be seen as one element in a campaign to reduce the clout of unions in the United States and force the majority of workers to accept lower living standards. Demands for givebacks and sophisticated union-busting efforts are part of the same

campaign, as are efforts to weaken environmental regulations and workplace standards for health and safety.

Does industry have to leave the United States?

Corporate executives maintain that the global factory and the loss of U.S. jobs it entails are an inevitable development. U.S. workers, they say, have "priced themselves out of the market," and so U.S. plants cannot stand up to foreign competition.

Profit rates for U.S.-owned corporations have been falling steadily since the 1970s. In many cases, the differences in labor costs between the United States and the Third World are so great that no changes in management or technology could compensate for them and still enable U.S.-based TNCs to maintain the high profits they want. Rather than accept the corporate view that U.S. workers are overpaid, we might ask: how much is too much? Did anyone ever say that a plant had to close because management wanted too much profit?

If the goal is economic viability rather than high profits, there are ways for manufacturing firms to improve productivity while remaining in the United States. Privately owned companies could focus on combatting mismanagement or making greater investments in research and development, rather than seeing lowered wages as the only route to cost cutting. In addition, in many areas groups have formed to promote worker buyouts or community ownership of enterprises. This approach offers the possibility of developing human and community resources that are critical to a healthy economy.

Today, workers in many basic industries are being pressured to accept unprecedented wage cuts. But concessions bring no guarantee that plants will stay open. In many cases, the companies take the money they have saved and invest it in totally unrelated enterprises, like financing mergers. Corporate profits go up, and the plants close anyway. As long as businesses seek the highest possible profits, regardless of other considerations, shutdowns and economic dislocation are the inevitable result.

What are some of the larger implications of the global factory?

What TNCs are aiming for is nothing less than a restructuring of the U.S. workforce.

Wages are falling steeply in heavy industry, which has traditionally paid the highest wages in manufacturing. Meanwhile, deep cuts in almost every social program are creating another kind of downward pressure on living standards, as poverty deepens for members of marginalized groups. When working people in general are less well off, the overall bargaining power of labor is greatly reduced.

As the unionized sector contracts, what is known as the "informal" sector of the economy is growing rapidly. Researcher Patricia Fernandez Kelly, widely known for her work on the *maquiladora* system in Mexico, has also studied the situation of immigrant women in the garment industry in border states like Florida or California. "The garment industry," she says, "has been portrayed as the epitome of an industry in decline. In fact, it is not declining—it is going underground."

In some parts of the country, like the Northeast or the Midwest, many garment manufacturers have closed down. In areas like Los Angeles, however, illegal homework and underground sweatshops are taking the place of legal factories that can be held accountable to labor standards. The workers are mostly undocumented immigrant women who face detention and deportation if they try to stick up for their rights.

Fernandez Kelly sees what she calls a trend toward the "Third World-ization" of the United States. She cites the example of "urban enterprise zones," which have been advocated by industrial development experts in several states and are already in place in some depressed areas in Connecticut or the South Bronx. Essentially, these zones would be like Third World export processing zones, located in U.S. urban ghettoes where chronic unemployment is at its worst. In the name of job creation, minimum wage laws, labor standards, and environmental restrictions would be lifted.

Fernandez Kelly and many other observers believe that economic restructuring is closely related to the new immigration law enacted in 1987, known formally as the Immigration Reform and Control Act (IRCA). This law has provided a limited amnesty to fewer than two million undocumented immigrants. At the same time, it has crippled labor rights for those who did not attain legal status—a number estimated at three to six million people.

Indications are that one thing IRCA has *not* done is substantially reduce the number of undocumented workers in the United States. Now, however, they face deportation if they protest any form of mistreatment by bosses or other authorities. Before IRCA, a series of court decisions had affirmed the right of undocumented workers to be protected by the same labor standards as all U.S. workers. Union organizing drives were also protected.

By criminalizing the undocumented, IRCA wipes out those protections and increases the incentives for more employment to go underground. From this perspective, the new immigration law works to lower living standards for all U.S. working people by driving down wages and working conditions for the most vulnerable groups.

Economic restructuring is also related to racism in two important ways. One concerns the overall cultural atmosphere in U.S. society. As economic dislocation increases, so do racist violence and hatred. White supremacist organizations like the Ku Klux Klan encourage white workers to blame their problems and vent their rage on African-Americans and other people of color, as well

JIM WEST/IMPACT VISUALS

as immigrants, Jews, and Arabs. Every available study shows that racist violence—like violence directed against lesbian/gay people—is increasing sharply.

Second, racism is involved on a more structural level. Blacks, Latinos, and Asians—like undocumented workers—are generally employed in certain types of jobs. After World War II, for example, upward mobility for African-Americans was closely tied to their entry into industrial jobs. Now, many employers are leaving areas where African-American workers are concentrated. As a result, African-Americans are increasingly excluded from stable employment, and the gap between white and Black living standards is widening.

The economics of immigration and racism are extremely complex and cannot be fully described in this guide. Experiences are different for each racial or ethnic group and for women and men within each group. A more detailed analysis may be found in some of the resources for further study listed in chapter 7.

What can we do about the global factory?

In this chapter we have painted a grim picture of economic deterioration at home, coupled with deepening poverty abroad. The problems posed by TNCs are indeed very great. But labor and other social movements are fighting back, in both the United States and the Third World. Already, such movements have many victories they can point to.

Individually, none of these movements has enough power to stand up successfully to the transnationals or demand changes in government policies that promote the export of jobs. In coalition, however, their power is far greater. And by building ties with similar movements in Third World countries, they can undermine one of the TNCs' greatest advantages: their ability to play off workers in different parts of the world against each other.

Through the media—which is itself dominated by major transnational corporations—people in the United States are subtly encouraged to blame immigrants and foreign workers for the loss of their jobs and the decline in their standard of living. But in the global economy, it is TNCs that call the shots, not workers in other countries. Resentment of foreign or foreign-born workers cannot bring about any improvements in our situation. That can occur only when working people demand a say in economic decisions that affect our lives so deeply.

The bulk of this guide explores how different movements are taking action on the global factory. Chapter 2 explores the movement against plant closings in the United States. Next, chapters 3 and 4 profile workers' movements in two Third World countries: Mexico and the Philippines. Chapter 5 surveys the many different ways that U.S. groups are reaching out to build international networks.

A Note on Sources

Information in this chapter is drawn from the files of AFSC's Women and Global Corporations Project, as well as from many of the pamphlets and books listed in chapter 7. Additional published sources include:

"The Impact of the Latin American Debt Crisis on the U.S. Economy," U.S. Congress, Joint Economic Committee, 1986.

"Runaway Shops and Female Employment: The Search for Cheap Labor" by Helen Safa, *Signs: Journal of Women in Culture and Society* 7:2, Winter 1981.

"The Subordination of Women and the Internationalization of Factory Production," Diane Elson and Ruth Pearson, in *Women, Households, and the Economy,* Rutgers University Press, 1988.

2. Plant Closings in the United States

In the spring and summer of 1988, the issue of plant closings in the United States burst into public awareness on an unprecedented scale. During the primary season, Democratic presidential contender Jesse Jackson traveled the country denouncing corporate "merging and purging"—the mass layoffs that have so often resulted from the wave of corporate takeovers during the 1980s. As a major trade bill worked its way through Congress, a provision requiring a sixty-day advance notice of plant shutdowns received extensive media attention. The bill was a number one priority for organized labor, and it also had broad popular support. The plant-closings language was passed by Congress, vetoed by outgoing president Ronald Reagan, and passed again as a separate bill. By August, Reagan had backed down from his announced intention to use his veto a second time, reportedly under heavy pressure from Republican candidates fearful of a backlash at the polls. An advance-notice requirement—which had been introduced repeatedly in Congress since 1974—had finally become law.

While the new law is a step forward, it is far from a solution. For one thing, most plant-closings activists say, sixty days is far too short a period for workers and their communities to respond to a shutdown with much effect. The bill as passed was drastically watered down from earlier proposals for a one-year advance notice requirement, extended health insurance, retraining benefits, and the like. Then, once the battle in Congress was over, plant closings quickly faded from the national media.

In many ways, though, the media were overlooking the real story. The deeper meaning of all this legislative maneuvering is that public concern over plant closings can no longer be discounted. In 1988's election-year news coverage, the scores of grassroots campaigns against shutdowns by unions and community groups were essentially invisible.

Yet it is these efforts, more than anything else, that have forced the issue onto the national stage. The overwhelming popular response to Jesse Jackson's message has also underlined the urgency of the problem for millions of U.S. working people.

The advance-notice law was the first major victory for the plant-closings movement on a national level. When attention is focused on locally based campaigns around plant closings, there are many other noteworthy advances to report. To list only a few:

• A major focus of the plant-closings movement has been "runaway shops," or the flight of jobs within the United States. In Duluth, Minnesota, in mid-1988, the Triangle Corp. was ordered by a state district judge to return more than $450,000 worth of machinery it had moved from its Duluth plant to a nonunion plant in Orangeburg, South Carolina. In their suit against Triangle, the union and the Duluth city govern-

Detroit, 1987: Jesse Jackson speaks to a rally against plant closings attended by auto workers from around the midwest.

ment charged that the firm had planned to shut down its Duluth plant when it asked the city for a $10-million industrial-revenue bond, promising to expand employment. The case is still being fought out on appeal.

Other suits on similar grounds have been filed or threatened in communities ranging from Clarksburg, West Virginia, to Kenosha, Wisconsin, to Freehold, New Jersey. In several cases such actions have forced the companies involved—which include giants like Chrysler and General Motors—to fund transitional assistance packages and make other concessions.

• In recent years, labor activists have developed a new strategy of analyzing early warning signals of an impending plant shutdown, allowing unions and workers' groups to uncover management's intentions long enough in advance to mobilize community support and organize an effective campaign. In some instances, early warning campaigns have been able to preserve jobs; in others, workers have negotiated substantially better severance packages and transitional support services.

• In 1988, community-based plant-closings groups from around the country joined together to form their first national network—the Federation for Industrial Retention and Renewal (FIRR). Such a network will enable small local groups to share information and insights with their counterparts from other areas. FIRR will work to help new groups get started, especially in the South and Southwest. It can also help to promote national policy initiatives that are based in experiences and perspectives from the grass-roots.

While it is vital to emphasize these success stories, it is equally important to recognize that the plant-closings movement faces a thorny problem indeed. So far, no strategy has had much success in halting or reversing *deindustrialization*—that is, the withdrawal of capital investment from industry in the United States. As described in chapter 1, this trend is part of the overall restructuring of the global economy under the domination of transnational corporations (TNCs).

Today, in most cases, plant-closings groups are fighting for more favorable terms for workers affected by shutdowns. Campaigns that succeed in entirely averting a closure are rare. At this stage, the main issue is one of demanding greater accountability from corporations, rather than a change of direction in basic economic trends.

In this chapter we offer more detail on plant closings in the United States, exploring the roots of the problem and how workers and their communities are responding. For those who wish to study the issue in depth, further readings are listed as resources in chapter 7.

9.7 MILLION LOST JOBS

In the five years from 1983 to 1988—the longest peacetime economic expansion in U.S. history—9.7 million workers lost their jobs through plant losings or layoffs.

As of January 1988, 30% remained unemployed among those counted officially as displaced workers—the 4.7 million who had held their jobs for three years or more. Nearly half of those with new jobs took pay cuts, with deep cuts of 20% or more reported for 30% of the re-employed.

Source: Bureau of Labor Statistics

MORE THAN TWO MILLION JOBS A YEAR

How serious is the problem of plant closings in the U.S. economy?

The most reliable statistics on the extent of plant closings come from a survey conducted by the federal Bureau of Labor Statistics (BLS) in 1984 and updated in 1986. The survey found that during the five years from January 1981 to January 1986, 10.8 million workers lost their jobs as a result of "plant closures, abolition of positions or shifts, or slack work." According to the Full Employment Action Council, more than two million workers, or 2.5 percent of the workforce, are affected each year. These displaced workers account for between a quarter and a third of all adult unemployment.

Although the phenomenon of deindustrialization can be traced back to the mid-1960s, it was during the 1970s that it became a major national problem. In the course of that decade, between 32 and 38 million jobs were lost to the U.S. economy, according to researchers Barry Bluestone and Bennett Harrison in their comprehensive 1982 book, *The Deindustrialization of America*.

Who is affected by plant closings?

According to the BLS survey, 65 percent of displaced workers were men and 35 percent were women. The racial breakdown was 87 percent white and 11 percent Black. Latino workers accounted for 6 percent of the total. (Because government figures consider race and "Hispanic origin" as separate categories, Latinos are included in the figures for both whites and Blacks. Figures for other racial groups were not given.) The proportion of displaced women workers was significantly higher among African-Americans, standing at 46 percent.

One problem with these statistics is that the more detailed analysis, including race and gender breakdowns, covers only workers who had held their jobs for at least three years before being laid off. This group included only 5.1 million workers—less than half of the original total. By limiting its in-depth findings to the smaller group, the BLS survey masks the experiences of workers who have had long-term difficulty in finding stable employment. In other words, the BLS decided not to study workers affected by the logic of "last hired, first fired"—who are far more likely to be women and people of color. Thus, the percentages given for these groups are too low.

Also, as noted in chapter 1, the BLS does not even count smaller shops, which predominate in certain industries (such as light manufacturing) and regions (such as the South). This further distorts the accuracy of our picture of who is affected by plant closings.

About half of the displaced workers in the BLS survey—49 percent—worked in the manufacturing sector, even though less than 20 percent of the country's labor force is employed in manufacturing. Three-quarters of displaced workers were in the prime working ages of 25 to 54 years. These figures also apply only to those who had held their job for at least three years before losing it.

JIM WEST/IMPACT VISUALS

How easy is it for dislocated workers to find another job?

Of the 5.1 million workers selected for the more detailed analysis, 33 percent were without work at the time of the BLS survey (January 1986). Another 10 percent were working at part-time jobs, even though the vast majority had held full-time jobs before being laid off.

The median time spent unemployed was eighteen weeks. However, 18 percent were unemployed for six months to a year, and 19 percent for more than a year. Many of those in this last category simply left the paid labor force. Of those displaced workers who received unemployment benefits, half exhausted them before they found another job. Of those who found another full-time job, 27 percent took pay cuts of more than 20 percent. Many also had difficulty in finding stable employment; 29 percent reported that

they had held two or more jobs since their layoff. Other studies have shown reduced income levels persisting for many workers for as long as six years after a layoff.

Re-employment was significantly more difficult for women and people of color. Among white men, 72 percent had found another job by the time of the BLS survey. This figure fell to 64 percent for Latino men, 60 percent for white women, 58 percent for African-Americans (both men and women), and a shockingly low 42 percent for Latina women. Re-employment rates were also much lower for older workers and less skilled workers.

What is the impact of plant closings on families and communities?

A number of studies have documented the devastating effects of plant closures on the health and family life of displaced workers.

Economically strapped families cut their spending on such basic necessities as housing, food, and health care. Some lose their homes to mortgage foreclosures.

Shutdowns are commonly accompanied by a rise in serious health problems, including cirrhosis, heart disease, and high blood pressure. Rates increase for alcoholism, depression, and mental illness. One study found displaced workers committing suicide at thirty times the expected rate. Many researchers have found increases in domestic violence and child abuse. Rates also rise for crimes outside the family group.

Communities face a serious strain as the demand for all kinds of social services increases while tax revenues drop. When the plant that closes is particularly large, or when it is the main source of employment in a community, an entire town can be devastated as the effects ripple through the local economy. Small businesses suffer as their customers cut back on consumption. According to estimates cited by Bluestone and Harrison, two service-sector jobs are lost every time three jobs disappear in the manufacturing sector.

When entire industries are affected by deindustrialization, the same dynamic occurs on a regional or a national scale. Supplier industries lay off additional workers as their sales drop. For the auto industry, for example, various studies have shown that one to two manufacturing jobs are lost in the supplier network for each auto job lost.

The Midwest Center for Labor Research (MCLR) has analyzed the social impact of numerous plant closures, often to provide an organizing tool to unions and community groups. These studies use existing research to project how many workers will be unemployed over a two-year period, the wage cuts they are likely to take in a new job, the indirect effects of the closure on suppliers and local merchants, and so on.

In 1988, for example, MCLR prepared a social impact study for the Cleveland Plant Closing Coalition on the effects of shutting down the city's LTV Steel plant. The resultant layoff of nearly 7000 workers, according to MCLR, would impose costs over a two-year period of $79.3 million in lost federal income taxes, $20 million in lost state taxes, $34.6 million in lost Social Security revenue, and $3.9 million in lost sales taxes. At the same time, the closure would require expenditures of $75.7 million in unemployment compensation and $10.6 million in welfare payments. Thus, the total price tag for that single shutdown would be more than $224 million.

Other effects on the community are not so easy to put into numbers. For example, people facing long-term unemployment attend churches and synagogues less often, are less likely to vote, and generally stop participating in community life. A reduced tax base can mean serious declines in the quality of all public services—from schools to highway maintenance to police and fire protection.

What is the impact of plant closings on labor unions?

So far, there have been no definitive studies of the overall impact of shutdowns on labor unions. However, there are ample indications that plant closings bear a large share of the responsibility for the serious decline in the extent of unionization in the United States. In 1954, the portion of unionized jobs in the United States stood at 35 percent. By 1978, that figure had fallen to 21 percent; by 1985, to 15 percent.

In California, according to researcher Anne Lawrence, union jobs in manufacturing dropped by nearly 19 percent between 1979 and 1983. Eighty-eight percent of this loss was caused by layoffs and plant closures in which union members lost their jobs. In other words, the decline in union membership is not occurring because U.S. workers are leaving unions, but because union workers are losing their jobs.

The United Auto Workers union (UAW) reports that its membership dropped from 1.3 million in 1978 to 920,000 in 1983. By

Auto battery worker exposed to lead poisoning, Visalia, California.

EARL DOTTER

1987, membership had recovered somewhat, rising to 978,000. Even with this improvement, however, the union still faced a 26-percent loss in only nine years. Nearly all of this drop, the UAW believes, has been caused by structural changes in the auto industry that have resulted in plant closures and increased automation.

BEHIND THE WAVE OF DEINDUSTRIALIZATION

Why do plants close?

Plant closings may have many immediate causes—a corporate merger, a decision to move a plant to another region or country, a failing business, or the like. When it comes to the underlying reasons for the extensive plant closures of the past twenty years, there are various conflicting theories. Not surprisingly, the explanation that is chosen depends on the point of view of those doing the explaining.

Conservative economists often blame excessive taxation, high wages, and environmental restrictions for undermining U.S. "competitiveness." In their view, deregulation will pave the way for a renaissance of U.S. industry. Some argue that a certain amount of turnover is essential as older industries become obsolete and newer ones take their place. Any attempt to slow the process, they say, would simply reduce the overall economic welfare of the United States.

More progressive analysts counter that neither deregulation nor deindustrialization has actually led to any growth in domestic industrial jobs. The huge corporate tax reductions enacted during the Reagan Administration—which were supposed to stimulate investment and create jobs—have mainly been used to finance corporate mergers and acquisitions. The same is true of the cash that is generated by selling off or shutting down existing plants: it is used for financial speculation, not reindustrialization. In this regard, shutdowns are one consequence of the "merger mania" that is sweeping the U.S. economy.

When capital is reinvested in industry, often it is invested outside the United States. During the 1970s, for example, the General Electric Corporation increased its worldwide payroll by 5000 jobs. It accomplished this, however, by adding 30,000 jobs abroad and cutting out 25,000 jobs in the United States.

Alternatively, as noted earlier, investment may be shifted to lower-wage areas of the United States, especially areas where organized labor is weaker.

The international movement of jobs is discussed in detail in chapter 1. In the paragraphs that follow, we will briefly consider the two other main causes of plant closings: relocation within the United States and corporate financial speculation.

What is the impact of the movement of jobs within the United States?

Inside the United States, the mobility of jobs has caused considerable competition among state governments to attract or retain industry by lowering business taxes, easing zoning and environmental restrictions, providing highways, and the like. One effect of this trend, according to economists Bluestone and Harrison in *The Deindustrialization of America*, is that the differences in tax rates among different states have all but disappeared. In other words, no state has really been able to gain a competitive advantage in this way—but the corporations have been able to drive down the overall level of business taxes.

The frantic movement of jobs and capital from one place to another does lead to reindustrialization of a sort. However, although many jobs are moving to the South and Southwest, the gap between rich and poor is actually growing throughout the "Sunbelt." Other consequences of such uncontrolled industrialization include a severe crisis in affordable housing, water shortages, and other environmental problems. Low property taxes, enacted to attract industry, mean that local communities have far fewer resources for every type of public service—from police and fire protection to schools to mass transit.

For an older area like New England, meanwhile, high-tech industry is promoted

THE SHIFTING TAX BURDEN

In 1960, individual wage-earners contributed 53% of the federal government's income through income taxes and Social Security taxes. Sales taxes accounted for 19%, and taxes on corporate profits contributed 28%.

By 1983, the corporate share of the federal tax burden had fallen to 10%. Sales taxes now stood at 15% and individual wage earners were responsible for 75%.

Source: Center for Popular Economics

FEWER MANUFACTURING JOBS

Manufacturing jobs have fallen steadily as a percentage of total U.S. employment for the past forty years:

26% in 1950
25% in 1960
24% in 1970
20% in 1980
17% in 1986

Source: Center for Popular Economics

as the replacement for older industries like textiles or shoes that have largely closed down. Computer-related industries have created jobs directly and brought a host of new service-sector jobs in their wake, in banking, insurance, hotels, and the like. Yet, note Bluestone and Harrison, for the majority of people in the region, the overall consequences include lower wages, declining purchasing power, less stable employment, and cuts in public services. Here, too, there is a growing polarization between rich and poor.

All of these trends, in "Sunbelt" and "Frostbelt" alike, show striking similarities to the impact of transnational corporations (TNCs) on Third World development, which was described in chapter 1. In many ways, these same TNCs are now generating "underdevelopment" within the United States—just as they have for decades throughout the Third World.

What is the relationship between plant closings and corporate mergers?

In today's economy, corporations unquestionably have money to invest. More and more frequently, however, they are using their capital to finance mergers, rather than creating new productive capacity or modernizing older plants.

The number and size of corporate mergers have been rising since the end of World War II—and undergoing a wild acceleration in the current decade. The value of mergers that took place in 1985 was more than five times greater than it had been in 1975. Often, mergers are followed by shutdowns of entire operations and mass layoffs—partly because of the huge amounts of debt incurred in financing the merger.

Such financial maneuvering is increasingly driving out productive investment. A handbook by the Plant Closures Project, entitled *Plant Closures: Myths, Realities, Responses*, points out that in one recent year, corporations spent $73.1 billion on 2,533 mergers. In that same year, less than $1 billion was allocated to venture capital—that is, investment in new businesses.

Bluestone and Harrison observe that a plant closure is often just the final stage of a much broader process of disinvestment. The profits from one operation may be diverted to financing new acquisitions rather than maintaining or modernizing the plant that generated the profit. Corporations even

have a name for this process, which they term "milking" the assets of a "cash cow." After years of such treatment, management will claim it has no choice but to close the by-now unprofitable establishment.

In the 1980s, the growing phenomenon of leveraged buyouts has become another cause of shutdowns. A leveraged buyout is the acquisition of a corporation by its own management—using very small amounts of equity and very large amounts of debt financing, known as "junk bonds." Once the deal is concluded, the new owners have a huge debt to pay off—increasing the pressure to strip the assets of profitable operations.

Large, diversified corporations may also close a profitable operation, simply because it is not profitable enough. Bluestone and Harrison speak of "hurdle rates of return," or minimum profit targets for all of a firm's holdings. Often these rates are well above the average profit rate for the industry involved. Any establishment that does not meet the target, however viable it may be, is simply disposed of.

The number of plant shutdowns has accelerated as more and more industries have been swallowed up by conglomerates, composed of many unrelated businesses joined in a single corporate entity. Conglomerates have no stake in the future of any particular industry; short-term profit maximization is their overriding goal. The plant-closures "early warning" movement mentioned earlier in this chapter considers that whenever a plant is acquired by a conglomerate, that in itself is a warning signal of a possible shutdown.

What are some of the political motivations for deindustrialization?

Despite the prevailing corporate view that U.S. workers earn too much, in fact, as noted in chapter 1, the real wages of U.S. working people have been declining steadily for more than fifteen years. Similarly, corporate complaints about high taxes do not stand up under examination. The corporate share of the federal tax burden fell from around 28 percent in the 1950s to 12 percent in 1980. With the tax reform of 1981, corporate contributions to federal revenues dropped even further, to 7.5 percent.

Chapter 1 of this guide described how all the changes going on in the U.S. economy are interrelated. High-paying jobs are disappearing from traditional industrial strongholds. When the jobs reappear—whether in another state or in another country—wage levels are much lower. Most new jobs are in the lower-paying service sector, and many of them offer only part-time work without benefits.

As we have seen, unions have been deeply hurt by the erosion of industry. Further, they are constantly under attack—in the media as well as at the bargaining table. The declining influence of unions has reduced the bargaining power of working people as a whole. At the same time, deep cuts in social programs have weakened the social "safety net." The combined result of these trends is that more people are forced by desperation to take any job they can, however poor the wages and working conditions.

Many observers do not believe that deindustrialization is just the result of economic forces, operating blindly without human choice. Rather, they see deindustrialization as a conscious corporate strategy. The goal of this strategy is to drive down wages and living standards for most U.S. working people, in order to increase corporate profits. This viewpoint is explained in more detail in chapter 1.

UNIONS AND COMMUNITIES RESPOND

How has organized labor responded to plant closures?

Unions have used a broad range of tactics in attempting to preserve the jobs of their members. In the 1980s, job security has become the highest priority in collective bargaining agreements. A few unions have negotiated an outright ban on plant closures or relocations for the period of the contract. Many contracts require employers to notify the union of a shutdown as much as six months in advance. With hopes of improving job security, some unions have also agreed to concessions or "givebacks," including deep wage cuts and changes in work rules.

Unfortunately, job security has proven an elusive goal for labor unions. Researcher Anne Lawrence, studying the experience of California manufacturing unions, found that job security provisions in union contracts did not actually improve the job security of union members. Concessions also did not improve the picture. Except in a few isolated instances, collective bargaining has been unable to keep plants from closing.

On the other hand, unions have frequently been successful in cushioning workers against economic dislocation. Many contracts, for example, require benefits for displaced workers, which may include severance payments, early retirement, extended medical benefits, retraining programs, and transfer to other company facilities. Collective bargaining, Lawrence states, has "clearly benefited dislocated workers."

To improve their ability to fight plant closings, unions, especially at the local level, have adopted a variety of innovative approaches. Some have focused on direct action, through shop-floor tactics like early warning systems. Others have joined forces with community-based and church-based groups, launching grassroots campaigns to halt shutdowns. Still others have turned to political action, pressing for legislation to regulate plant closures and new public policies to promote industrial renewal. Each of these approaches is discussed in more detail below.

What is an early warning system?

When a plant is preparing to shut down, normally the company tries to keep its plans a secret. For workers and their communities, on the other hand, the sooner they know about a shutdown, the better they can prepare to fight it. In recent years, plant-closings activists have developed considerable expertise in spotting signs of an impending shutdown.

An *Early Warning Manual* published by the Midwest Center for Labor Research (MCLR) lists ten long-term indicators of a potential plant closing. These include ownership problems (including acquisition by a conglomerate), disinvestment, declining sales and employment, mismanagement, duplicate capacity, management instability, changes in land use, complaints about the "business climate," inadequate research and development, and changes in management behavior.

MORE SERVICE JOBS

Employment in lower-paying service jobs has been rising rapidly as a percentage of total U.S. employment:

28% in 1950
32% in 1960
39% in 1970
43% in 1980
49% in 1986

Source: Center for Popular Economics

**THE
UNEMPLOYMENT
INSURANCE GAP**

The coverage offered by unemployment insurance has contracted sharply in recent years. The figures below show the percentage of unemployed workers receiving unemployment compensation in typical years:

49.7% in 1959
41.6% in 1969
42.1% in 1979
31.5% in 1988

Source: Center on Budget and Policy Priorities

Signs that a shutdown is an immediate threat include removal of equipment, evidence of a cash crunch, unusual bargaining positions in contract negotiations, cosmetic improvements to the plant, and delinquencies in property taxes.

Based on the experience of numerous local groups, MCLR's manual describes how to tap varied sources of information—on the shop floor, in the community, and even from sympathetic management employees. Early warning empowers workers to take action before a shutdown is unavoidable—including seeking a buyer for the plant, exploring the feasibility of a worker buyout, and mobilizing public opinion against the shutdown. Some local groups have been able to win the support of community leaders and public officials by documenting a company's secret plans to disinvest.

From 1982 to 1984, for example, Local 277 of the United Electrical Workers (UE) used early warning, a strike, and an active community campaign to prevent Gulf & Western from shutting down the Morse Cutting Tool plant in New Bedford, Massachusetts. When the city's mayor threatened to use the power of eminent domain to seize the plant, G&W was forced to keep Morse open for a year, and then sell instead of liquidating. When the buyer went bankrupt in 1987, UE and the community mobilized again to make sure that the plant was sold to someone who would keep it open. Some 375 jobs were saved through this campaign, one of the most successful in the history of the plant-closings movement.

What kinds of coalitions have emerged to fight plant closings?

Coalition-building is vital to successful plant-closing campaigns. In describing the Morse Cutting Tool campaign, the *Plant Closures* handbook quotes Ron Poineau, president of UE Local 277. "Without the support of the community," he comments, "forget it! Together we saved Morse for the city as well as for the workers."

Four kinds of constituencies are important members of such campaigns, according to Conrad Johnson, former coordinator of the Interfaith Economic Crisis Organizing Network. These four are labor unions, community groups, religious institutions, and local government. "When these four elements are joined," says Johnson, "they can ignite powerful forces in the community."

Nearly all plant-closings groups have a strong local focus. The paragraphs that follow describe the experience of three of these local organizations. Next, we will take a look at some current efforts to knit local groups into a national movement.

*The Mon Valley:
Steel Is the Backbone*

In the late 1970s and early 1980s, the domestic steel industry was targeted for disinvestment by Armco, LTV, U.S. Steel, and other corporate giants. Employment at the former U.S. Steel Corporation dropped from nearly 172,000 in 1980 to 80,000 in 1984. Steel employment overall fell by 40 percent between 1980 and 1986.

In a supposed effort to save the steel industry, U.S. Steel reaped $850 million in federal tax breaks in 1981 and $3 billion in concessions from the steelworkers union in 1983. However, in the classic pattern of conglomerates, the company used the cash to finance acquisitions in unrelated businesses—including oil, plastics, chemicals, and real estate. In 1983, the company's chairman, David Roderick, said to angry steelworkers that "U.S. Steel is not in the business of making steel. It is in the business of making money." Shortly thereafter, the firm's name was changed to USX.

Meanwhile, such massive unemployment has had a devastating effect on the industry's traditional center—the tri-state region of eastern Ohio, western Pennsylvania, and northern West Virginia. In response, religious leaders, steelworkers and other trade unionists, community activists, and unemployed workers joined together to form the Tri-State Conference on Steel in 1979.

Tri-State's core strategy has been the promotion of community ownership and control of steel facilities. The group has also battled the closure of steel mills, fought for extended unemployment and medical benefits for displaced workers, and set up food banks. But its vision has always been centered in the belief that steel is the backbone of any industrial economy, as well as the basis of the region's prosperity. If the private sector won't modernize and operate the country's steel mills, Tri-State argues, local communities should step in.

In 1986, Tri-State was victorious in a lengthy campaign to establish a Steel Valley Authority (SVA) in Pennsylvania's Mon Valley. This public agency, supported by local municipalities, is empowered to take over plants using eminent domain when private owners refuse to keep them open. (Eminent domain is the power the government has traditionally used to take over property needed for highways and other "public purposes." In such takeovers, the owner of the property is compensated for its fair market value.)

With the SVA, the concept of eminent domain was extended for the first time to industrial planning and development. Plants acquired by the SVA can be sold to suitable private buyers—or to worker-owned or publicly owned industrial cooperatives. Accountability to local governments is built into the SVA governance structure.

The SVA does have its flaws. A 1988 discussion paper from Tri-State notes that "the entrenched conservatism of local municipalities" makes true community control difficult to achieve. Nonetheless, Tri-State believes, the SVA experience could serve as a model for a national response to deindustrialization.

Oakland, California:
A Broad Vision of Economic Justice

In 1987, the Oakland-based Congress for Economic Justice (CEJ) was launched. Its goal was to address many different aspects of economic crisis—ranging from plant closings to homelessness to youth unemployment.

In recent years, notes a CEJ statement, Oakland has lost more than 20,000 jobs—in retailing and the service sector as well as in manufacturing. In Oakland, as in many communities, shutdowns have had a devastating impact throughout the economy—not just on better-paying jobs in heavy industry.

Most of CEJ's demands are similar to those of other groups we have mentioned—including calls for a publicly funded early-warning system, stronger retraining and job-placement programs, and an industrial authority modeled on the SVA. However, the coalition's agenda is also broader than that of many other plant-closings groups. CEJ's Economic Bill of Rights calls for an increase in the minimum wage to $5.25, redirection of the local economy away from the military, no trade-offs of workplace health and safety or environmental protection in return for jobs, and support for strong affirmative action programs.

By broadening its concerns, CEJ speaks to the overall impact of economic dislocation on workers at all levels of the economy. This diversity is also reflected in CEJ's membership—which includes groups concerned with immigrant and minority communities, women's issues, peace, and housing, as well as religious, labor, and civic organizations.

CEJ grew out of years of organizing by Oakland's Plant Closures Project (PCP), which has included assistance to workers fighting specific shutdowns as well as broader community action and education. Many PCP-supported campaigns have targeted companies with a workforce that is predominantly women of color, including recent immigrants. Their stories highlight how race and gender influence the experience of economic dislocation.

Since 1986, for example, PCP has worked with community groups and Local 29 of the Office and Professional Employees Union (OPEU) to fight the relocation of hundreds

JIM WEST/IMPACT VISUALS

of clerical jobs at Blue Cross of California from Oakland to a nonunion location in suburban southern California. The campaign has exposed and slowed Blue Cross's efforts and won severance, retraining, and rehire rights for displaced workers.

In Oakland—where Blue Cross had been headquartered since 1936—nearly all of the workers were women. A large majority were African-American or Filipina, and many were single heads of households. Of 1100 workers in the OPEU bargaining unit in 1985, most earned between $7 and $9.75 per hour—wages comparable to those of a mid-level factory job.

Blue Cross's move, notes an OPEU report, is typical of trends within the insurance industry. Like other large-scale clerical employers, insurance companies are moving out of urban areas. For such firms, observes the report, "the 'preferred' workforce is predominantly white suburban housewives," who are presumed to be dependent on a husband's income. Such women are considered less likely to join unions and fight for higher wages.

The Plant Closures Project has been involved in numerous other campaigns around specific closures. It has also helped to secure the passage of several local and state laws regulating shutdowns. It has developed the *Plant Closures* handbook and other educational materials, as well as training programs. Like the Tri-State Conference on Steel, it is a leader in current efforts to build a national plant-closings movement.

North Carolina:
Organizing the Unorganized

In the stories we have considered so far, union locals have been major actors in plant-closing campaigns. What happens to workers who are not represented by a union when they are faced with a closure? The case of the Schlage Lock plant near Rocky Mount, North Carolina, provides an example of a successful campaign by a nonunion workforce.

The "phase-down" of Schlage Lock was announced long in advance—in October 1986, more than a year and a half before the scheduled closure. Workers were laid off gradually beginning in January 1987. By June 1988, only seventy-five remained out of a workforce of 683.

Schlage Lock, a subsidiary of the transnational Ingersoll-Rand Corporation, manufactures door locks and security systems. In the Rocky Mount plant, three-quarters of

the production workers were African-American; three-quarters were women. In announcing the shutdown, management said that production was being transferred to a new Schlage plant in Tecate, Mexico, and a recently expanded plant in Colorado Springs.

In October 1986, management indicated that details would be forthcoming on severance pay and stay-in-place bonuses. In January 1988, however, production workers learned that they would receive no severance and only a one-month extension of their health coverage. White-collar employees, on the other hand, were receiving both severance benefits—one week's pay for each year worked—and six months of extended health insurance.

Angered by this unequal treatment, workers turned to two local groups for assistance: Southerners for Economic Justice and Black Workers for Justice. With their help, laid-off and current employees organized the Committee Against Schlage Lock Plant Closing in March 1988.

Health and environmental issues were another key focus of the group's concerns. Members of the Schlage committee say at least seventeen workers have died of cancer in the last few years, and many suffer from chronic respiratory conditions and other problems. When the Schlage committee sponsored a health screening of eighty workers, dozens were found to be suffering from symptoms of toxic exposure. Hundreds of drums of toxic wastes have been stored at the plant, and illegal dumping was revealed at a public meeting by a worker who was ordered to do it. In the wake of this admission, tests by state officials have found significant levels of cancer-causing chemicals and heavy metals in the groundwater for half a mile around.

The Schlage committee turned to the local community for support, organizing prayer breakfasts, public hearings, a petition campaign, pickets, and other actions. A leaflet publicizing the toxic waste problem was distributed to homes near the plant. In the end, the company agreed to give the workers pension benefits and half the severance pay they were demanding. Schlage also promised to provide thorough medical exams for all the workers and to clean up the contamination around the plant.

The campaign gave rise to a permanent organization, now known as Schlage Workers for Justice. Beyond these specific achievements, the experience netted "many gains in consciousness," observes Leah Wise of Southerners for Economic Justice (SEJ). The

Schlage workers contacted Hometowns Against Shutdowns, a national resource center, and learned they were eligible for benefits under the Trade Readjustment Act, which covers workers displaced by foreign economic competition. "In this case," reports Wise, "the government deemed Schlage Lock to be its own competition, because they were opening a plant in Mexico." As a result, 104 workers are receiving training and relocation benefits.

'This was the first time the Trade Readjustment Act was utilized in North Carolina," adds Wise, "which is mind-boggling when you consider the number of plants that have closed here." SEJ plans to continue working to build local campaigns against shutdowns—as well as bringing "a southern perspective," as Wise comments, to the national plant-closings movement.

JIM WEST/IMPACT VISUALS

How is the plant-closings movement developing nationally?

As noted at the beginning of this chapter, the plant-closings movement took a large step forward in 1988, with the formation of a network known as the Federation for Industrial Retention and Renewal (FIRR). This group grew out of a task force of the Interfaith Economic Crisis Organizing Network (IECON), which has worked since 1983 to bring together grassroots organizations concerned with economic dislocation.

With more than twenty organizational members, FIRR offers local groups a forum for sharing their experiences and discussing organizing strategies. At its April 1989 meeting, FIRR set up a staffed national office. With staff, FIRR could play an even stronger role in helping new plant-closings groups organize in local communities.

FIRR has already been able to play this kind of role more informally. For the Schlage Lock committee, comments Leah Wise, FIRR was "an enormous boon. The campaign could not have achieved so much in so short a time without this resource." Wise is a member of FIRR's steering committee.

The launching of FIRR is one of many signs that the plant-closings movement is "maturing," comments Jack Metzgar of the Midwest Center for Labor Research (MCLR). "We've had more victories and close calls recently. We've moved from protesting shutdowns to feasibility studies for worker buyouts or community ownership. It's a whole different fight than it was five years ago."

Still, Metzgar concedes, the number of jobs that have been saved through plant-closing campaigns is minuscule, in most cases numbering in the hundreds—while millions of jobs have been lost to deindustrialization. "Decisions at the national level," according to Metzgar, "make it impossible for purely local struggles to succeed."

MCLR is one of several FIRR members that believe the group should also fight for national legislation designed to combat deindustrialization. Although various policy proposals have been discussed within the movement, so far there is no broad consensus on the best approach to take.

Aside from its limited material gains, the plant-closings movement has had an important impact on public awareness of the causes of plant closures. "In key industrial communities," states Metzgar, "we have reversed the public perception that nothing can be done." This, he believes, may be the movement's most important contribution so far.

What challenges face the plant-closings movement?

To continue to grow, the plant-closings movement needs to bring together many diverse constituencies, some of which have little history of cooperation. A common strategy can only emerge from the cross-fertilization of many different perspectives and experiences. Fostering this kind of exchange is a major goal of groups like FIRR and IECON.

The vital connection between unions and community groups, for example, has often been a fragile one. While union locals have been deeply involved in many plant-closings campaigns, observes Jack Metzgar, unions at the regional and national levels have been slow to follow their lead. Few plant-closings groups have built a relationship with unions that extends beyond a specific campaign.

Health and safety and environmental issues are another challenge. How will the movement respond to "environmental blackmail"—that is, offers by corporations to retain or create jobs if worker safety and environmental controls are sacrificed? Some activists see this as an issue with the potential to split the movement for industrial renewal.

Several activists also stress the need for the plant-closings movement to develop ties with workers' groups from Third World countries. "We have very little sense of international connection," says Metzgar. "Many of us are involved as individuals in international solidarity work—especially around Central America—but the connections are not drawn to the global factory."

"If I had the resources," comments Leah Wise, "I'd be ferrying people back and forth from the Third World. Meeting other people who are struggling is one of the best strategies for organizing—it's an incredible eye-opener."

Some activists say that another challenge to the movement is the need for plant-closings groups to deepen their understanding of the impact of race and gender. "It used to be thought that the loss of manufacturing primarily affected white men," observes economist Teresa Amott. "Actually, Black communities have been the hardest hit. Manufacturing has been almost the only way a Black worker could make $12 an hour. Today, the fraction of adult Black men who are employed is frighteningly low." Amott is a member of IECON's executive committee.

Leah Wise stresses that the erosion of manufacturing is just one facet of the serious economic crisis within the African-American community. "Black women are facing the automation of clerical jobs and the flight of clerical employment to the suburbs," she points out. "Professionals are being devastated by cutbacks in government employment. Poor people are hit by cuts in public assistance. In the South, where Black people have been most likely to own land, that land is being lost. Our communities, our livelihood are being assaulted across the board."

At the same time, states Wise, "racism has seriously divided and weakened" progressive movements in the United States, "and as yet they have developed no strategic response."

With deindustrialization so far advanced, argues Amott, "the cutting edge of capital mobility" is in smaller, unorganized shops, often employing people of color, especially women. "We need to broaden our understanding of economic dislocation to include the experiences of these workers," Amott believes. "Today the most marginal industries are the front line, the place where capital is most willing to cut and run.

"Blacks, Latinos, Asians—each group of workers has its own particular experience, and that experience is different for men and women within each group. All of these conditions have important implications for what kind of strategies we will develop."

To encourage this kind of analysis within the plant-closings movement, Wise and Amott have worked to bring more women-of-color groups into IECON. "One organizer we heard from," recalls Wise, "represented a group known as Asian Immigrant Women Advocates (AIWA) in San Francisco. When she talked about her group's approach, she described how they work to give women the courage to say to their boss, 'please speak more slowly' or 'please don't yell at me.'

"A trade union organizer may never in their life have had to deal at that level. The institutional labor movement is used to working at the national policy level—but this

Auto foundry worker, Detroit.

EARL DOTTER

is the reality of where the unorganized sector is at.''

Amott notes that ''hearing from groups like AIWA gave many projects an appreciation of how much access they have—to policy makers, to funding, and to the resources of labor unions. They were stunned when they saw the lack of resources in which women's projects are operating—and amazed by the creativity they exhibit.''

Wise and Amott both believe that different organizing strategies are needed to reach out to women workers, especially in the unorganized sector. ''Women bring a holistic view of what organizing entails,'' says Wise. ''It touches on every aspect of people's lives. For women to organize frequently means profound changes in their self-concept, their family relationships—their entire lives. We need to talk about neighborhood and family issues as well as the workplace. And we need to use organizing approaches that focus on development—of our understanding, our skills, our organizations.''

Understanding race and gender, these activists believe, is vital if the plant-closings movement is to reach out to unorganized workers, who are a large majority of the TNC workforce.

TOWARD A NATIONAL INDUSTRIAL POLICY

Direct-action campaigns are vital to the empowerment of workers and their communities. To confront deindustrialization, however, most activists believe that it is also necessary to press for new public policies through legislation, rather than coping with shutdowns entirely on a case-by-case basis. This section takes a look at existing legislation and sketches in some of the proposals being made for alternative policies.

What is included in the 1988 advance-notice law?

The federal advance-notice law, which was passed in August 1988 and went into effect in February 1989, is formally known as the Worker Adjustment and Retraining Notification Act. It requires written notice of sixty days for any plant closing or mass layoff affecting more than fifty workers. The law applies to any company with 100 or more employees. The notice must be sent to the union, or, if there is no union, to each affected worker. The local government must also be notified, as well as the state office responsible for assisting dislocated workers under the Job Training Partnership Act.

Penalties for failing to give adequate notice include fines as well as full pay and benefits for each affected worker for the period of violation. Companies may be exempted from the sixty-day requirement if the shutdown or layoff was caused by ''business circumstances that were not reasonably foreseeable'' and in various other situations.

Activists stress that the law, while positive, is not enough. The notice period, in particular, is too short to allow workers and their communities time to mount an effective response. A statement from the Midwest Center for Labor Research comments that while the law ''is a humane measure which will materially benefit millions of dislocated workers, the need for vigilant early warning is as great as ever.''

Why has the requirement for advance notice of plant shutdowns been the centerpiece of national legislative efforts?

Common sense would suggest that the sooner workers and their communities learn of an impending plant shutdown, the better equipped they will be to deal with it. This assumption was documented in a comprehensive 1986 report by the Office of Technology Assessment (OTA), the research arm of Congress.

Workers who received advance notice, the OTA found, were more likely to receive severance benefits, participate in retraining programs, and find comparable new jobs. Advance notice gives unions, companies, and government agencies time to set up adjustment programs. It also gives workers a chance to think through their options and seek job counseling or other services.

ARE WOMEN'S WAGES RISING?

Women's earnings have increased considerably as a percentage of men's earnings in recent years. But only a small amount of the increase has occurred because women's wages are rising. The bulk of the change has come about because men's wages are falling.

In 1979, women earned, on the average, 62.6% of what men earned. By 1987, that figure had risen to 70.6%, an increase of 8 percentage points. If, however, men's wages had held steady at their 1979 level, women's wages in 1987 would have been only 65.5% of the figure for men—a far smaller gain of 2.9 percentage points.

Source: Economic Policy Institute

Unions can win better protection for their members with advance notice, according to the OTA report, especially when the term of the notice is longer. With a month's notice or less, few unions were able to negotiate a severance package. Unions that received notice of six months or more, however, were able to obtain severance pay and other benefits 80 percent of the time.

The OTA also examined the claims of business interests that advance notice will disrupt production as workers slow down, quality slips, and those with the highest level of skill leave to take new jobs. Laws calling for advance notice have been opposed almost universally on these grounds by business figures. However, the OTA could find no evidence of declines in either productivity or quality resulting from advance notice.

In fact, the OTA study found the opposite: workers often strive to produce more, better-quality goods, in hopes of persuading management to reconsider. In many cases, advance notice has also helped the companies themselves, winning them community goodwill and increased loyalty from remaining workers.

Despite its many benefits, advance notice was a rarity in the United States before it became federal law. The OTA study, released in late 1986, found that nearly a quarter of all workers who lost their jobs in a closure or mass layoff received no notice whatsoever. For those who did receive any warning, the average period was one week for blue-collar workers and two weeks for those in white-collar jobs—not much time to plan for the effects of losing a job! The only group that fared better were unionized workers, who received, on the average, seven times as much notice as their unorganized counterparts.

What other laws have been passed to regulate plant closings?

Only a few laws on plant closings have been enacted at the state and local level, and most are considerably weaker than the federal law. Maine, for example, requires severance pay and advance notice in the event of a closure or relocation—but the maximum penalty for a violation is $500. Connecticut calls for extension of health benefits for 120 days, but compliance is voluntary. Other states with some form of plant-closure law include Hawaii, Maryland, Massachusetts, Michigan, South Carolina, and Wisconsin.

Philadelphia is the only major city to have enacted such a law.

The Massachusetts law, passed in 1984, is often cited as a model because of its emphasis on prevention of shutdowns. For example, the law established a Product Development Corporation, which provides technical and financial assistance to stimulate new industrial opportunities. It also set up an Economic Stabilization Trust, which is a loan fund for economically viable but troubled businesses. Massachusetts also requires any business receiving public subsidies under these or other programs to adopt a voluntary "social compact," including advance notice of closures, extension of health benefits, and help to workers in finding new jobs.

For municipalities, an increasingly prominent tactic is the same "quid pro quo" approach of demanding some sort of accountability from corporations in return for public investments in the form of tax-exempt financing or other assistance. In New Haven, Connecticut, for instance, firms receiving public assistance must give the city six months' notice of any relocation.

This concept of corporate accountability in return for public investments and tax breaks is also being used in the courts, in the lawsuits mentioned earlier by the city of Duluth, Minnesota, and other towns.

How are plant closures handled in other parts of the advanced industrial world?

Before 1988's advance-notice law, the United States was the world's only advanced industrial nation without some sort of plant-closings policy. And, even though a U.S. law now exists, it is still the weakest.

In West Germany, for example, companies are required to give a year of advance notice. In Sweden, the period is six months. Japan relies on an elaborate system of cooperation among government, unions, and the corporate sector to plan orderly phase-outs of certain industries and retrain affected workers.

Most western European countries recognize the right of workers to have input into closure decisions. West German firms, for example, must consult with plant-based "works councils," which give workers a voice in decisions about layoffs and changes in production methods. When layoffs are contemplated, corporations must negotiate a "social plan" with their works councils to

COMPARING U.S. WAGES

The figures below present average total hourly labor costs (wages plus benefits) for the United States and some western European countries in 1988:

West Germany—
  $18.07
The Netherlands—
  $16.30
Denmark—$15.88
Belgium—$15.68
United States—$13.90
France—$12.99
Britain—$12.87
Ireland—$9.68
Spain—$8.75

Source: New York Times

minimize the economic and social dislocation. If a plan cannot be negotiated, the government's Labor Office steps in as a mediator. Even in Britain, where the notice period is only sixty days, corporations are required to consider union input on how many workers should be laid off and how the layoffs will be made.

As western Europe moves towards economic unification in 1992, many trade unionists fear an assault on their workplace rights and living standards because companies will be able to move more freely across national boundaries. Unions in West Germany or Scandinavia believe their jobs may flee to low-wage nations like Portugal. The unions are thus fighting for regulations designed to minimize this effect.

Already, some worker rights related to shutdowns have been recognized at the international level. Throughout the European Community (EC), collective-bargaining agreements remain in force whenever a corporation changes hands. Companies are required to give unions access to information about their economic health. When a firm goes bankrupt, EC nations must also give priority to claims by workers. None of these rights are recognized by U.S. law.

In the eyes of European trade unionists, however, even these relatively enlightened policies are insufficient. Workers' right to know what is going on in their industries is limited to the national level. Increasingly, however, the firms operating in European countries are the national subsidiaries of giant transnational corporations (TNCs).

Often, even the management of these subsidiaries is not fully informed about the plans being made in the TNC's home office.

Thus, in the 1980s, trade unionists have been fighting through such bodies as the European Parliament to require the same types of disclosure and advance notification from transnational corporate headquarters. Such proposals have been strenuously opposed by the TNCs, which see them as a first step in the direction of international collective bargaining.

What types of alternative policy proposals have been put forward in the United States?

More and more voices in society are agreeing that a systematic public policy is necessary to address the crisis of U.S. industry. TNCs have no commitment to the health of the U.S. economy or the well-being of U.S. workers. Yet economic security and stability are basic human rights that are desired by every group in society.

The term "economic planning" has long been taboo in the political culture of the United States, because it suggests that worst of all heresies—socialism. The myth is that no one plans the U.S. economy, that it is guided by impersonal "market forces." Yet it is obvious that a great deal of planning goes into economic decision-making. The difference is that the planning is in elite hands, and the process is not accountable to the public.

Garment workers in upstate New York.

EARL DOTTER

In fact, not just private corporations but also the federal government does a lot of economic planning. The Pentagon in particular is one of the most important planning agencies in the country—through its domination of research and development spending and enormous direct investments in military technology.

The fruits of the current U.S. approach to planning include deindustrialization, a shaky economy dominated by financial speculation, serious hardships for millions of dislocated workers, and a declining standard of living for nearly all of the country's working people. Today, more and more people are saying that's not a fair price to pay to keep corporate profits high.

Careful examination of alternative policy proposals is beyond the scope of this guide, but a few of the more common approaches should be mentioned. One such proposal calls for a system of regional job authorities (RJAs) similar to the Steel Valley Authority described above. These RJAs could intervene to prevent plant closures, if necessary acquiring plants by eminent domain and finding alternative owners.

A related proposal calls for a national industrial development fund—a federal agency that would provide capital for the revitalization of basic industry and coordinate national economic planning. Jesse Jackson and the Rainbow Coalition have proposed a national reinvestment bank, which would tap the resources of workers' pension funds to invest in reindustrialization projects.

One group has called for a new kind of "Superfund" that would provide wage replacement, job training, educational assistance, health insurance, and child-care services to assist dislocated workers in making the transition to new jobs. Others cite success stories in which worker ownership or even public ownership has kept certain enterprises running. Supporters of this approach call for publicly funded financial and technical assistance to facilitate worker buyouts. Still others argue that the first priority must be rebuilding the social "safety net," restoring the rights and protections that have been dismantled over the past decade.

Each of these approaches has its strengths, and each has weaknesses that must be confronted. At this stage, there is no clear consensus on a blueprint for economic renewal. A unifying strategy can only emerge from sustained organizing by a national movement with a strong grassroots base.

NO REAL VOICE

"The demand for an industrial policy is born from an understanding that the people of the United States have no real voice in shaping their economic destinies. Business decisions that determine the resources and futures of all Americans are made without reference to the desires or concerns of those people. These decisions are, in fact, often made without any reference to the needs of the nation or any community within the nation."

— Tri-State Conference on Steel

A Note on Sources

Background material for this chapter was compiled by Anne Lawrence and Jan Gilbrecht from the files of the Plant Closures Project in Oakland, CA. Key published sources include *The Deindustrialization of America* and the *Plant Closures Handbook,* both of which are listed in chapter 7. Additional information came from press reports of the 1988 battle for advance notification legislation and from interviews with plant closing activists.

Other published sources include:

Early Warning Manual Against Plant Closings, Midwest Center for Labor Research, revised 1988.

"Plant Closing: Advance Notice and Rapid Response," U.S. Congress, Office of Technology Assessment, 1986.

Plant Closings: Limited Advance Notice and Assistance Provided Dislocated Workers, U.S. General Accounting Office, July 1987.

"The Pulse of Economic Change: Displaced Workers of 1981-85," *Monthly Labor Review,* U.S. Bureau of Labor Statistics, June 1987.

Technology and Structural Unemployment: Reemploying Displaced Adults, U.S. Congress, Office of Technology Assessment, 1986.

3. The Mexican Maquiladoras

The *maquiladoras* have brought us nothing except jobs. But in solving the problem of employment, they create many more serious problems in our community and throughout the country. They create large concentrations of people—people for whom there is no adequate housing, public services, or transport. Women go out to work in the *maquiladoras* but they can't take proper care of their children because there are no daycare centers. In all of Juárez there are only three or four daycare centers for all those workers.

These are the words of Roberto,* a youthful garment worker in Ciudad Juárez, a city of 1.5 million people that lies just across the border from El Paso, Texas. With a *maquila* workforce of 120,000, Juárez is home to Mexico's largest concentration of *maquiladoras*, the U.S.-owned assembly plants that line the Mexico-U.S. border.

Mexican workers are concerned about conditions inside as well as outside the *maquila* plants. Luisa, a garment worker turned organizer, describes her experience in these words:

At Dimit [Farah] there are a lot of problems. There's no ventilation, no exhaust fans—even though there's a lot of dust in the factory. The dust came from the fabric that we were sewing. At the end of the day you would walk out of there covered with dust, all over your body. It caused a lot of illness. Headaches, sore throats, eye infections—all caused by the dust.

And Gloria, a veteran of electronics assembly work, reports:

There are an infinity of problems. Chemicals are spilled on the floor. Trays of solvents are left uncovered—methylene chloride [a known carcinogen], thinner, acetone, alcohol, flux. All these things are in the environment. In one job you measure the width of capacitors. On each tiny piece you take five or six measurements, making the same motion of your wrist all day long. Eventually the workers get a growth on their wrists and then they have to have an operation.

Low wages in the *maquiladoras*—currently around $23 a week—and harsh working conditions translate into a host of problems outside the workplace as well. As Roberto describes it,

Most of the workers live in conditions that have no dignity. They live in houses made out of adobe, scraps of wood, or even cardboard. They have to pay a lot just for water. They don't have electricity for lighting or other necessities. Without proper drainage, conditions are very unsanitary. You cannot drink the water, it is full of germs. People get sick from it. It's quite a contradiction. These companies arrive and say to the workers, "come and grow with us." But you can spend ten years working in the *maquiladoras* and you'll still be living in these same conditions.

For U.S. corporations, on the other hand, Mexico's desperate economic straits have proved a bonanza. With more than 1000 *maquila* plants, employing some 300,000 workers in all, Mexico now ranks first among developing countries in supplying cheap labor to U.S.-owned transnationals. The reason is not hard to find. Because of repeated devaluations of the peso beginning in 1982, Mexico's wage levels have become among the lowest in the world. In the ten years before 1983, the number of *maquilas* grew at an annual rate of 3.5 percent; since then the rate has jumped to 7.2 percent.

Some promotional literature from the Chamber of Commerce has also boasted of

---

* Where only first names are given, names have been changed to protect workers from reprisals.

the *maquilas*' ability to deliver a "strike-free workforce." On that count, at least, corporate optimism seems to be unfounded. Another worker-activist, Carmen, tells this story about a plant known as ECC (Electronics Control Corporation):

> Conditions used to be totally different. At one point they cut us back to four days a week. They said they couldn't get components because of problems in the United States. But we were working lots of overtime all the time. The workers formed a commission with a representative from each line and we demanded a five-day week and a 50 percent raise. Management said this was impossible. But we said, if there was a shortage of work how could there be so much overtime? In the end we won the five days and the 50 percent.

Carmen's story is not an unusual one. Formal strikes in the *maquilas* are still rare, but confrontations with management are increasingly common. And growing numbers of workers are becoming involved in small-scale but persistent battles over health and safety, wages and benefits, sexual harassment, and union democracy.

Although corporate literature is rife with references to the supposed "docility" of women workers—one reason they are considered more desirable for the *maquila* workforce—it is women who are taking the lead in demanding their rights. And it is women, too, who are taking the most initiative in seeking friends and allies on the other side of the border, drawing support from church, community, labor, and women's groups in the United States. Such efforts, while still in their infancy, could play a major role in strengthening the hand of labor and other constituencies against transnational corporations.

In the pages that follow, we will look in greater detail at how the *maquila* system works and its relationship to Mexico's overall economic situation. We will also take a look at the problems caused by *maquiladoras* for workers in both Mexico and the United States, and what people on both sides of the border are starting to do about these problems.

THE MAQUILADORA SCAM

"It's the biggest scam the world has ever seen. For U.S. firms to say, we have to leave the country in order to remain competitive—it's a con job. Politicians are participating in this scam, newspapers, chambers of commerce—they're all participating. The end result is that teenage girls are being exploited. A sixteen-, seventeen-year-old working in an assembly line? To me that's still a child—being exploited by Zenith, and RCA, and Sylvania, and all those textile firms."

—Union activist, El Paso, Texas

THE MAQUILADORA SYSTEM

Where did the *maquiladoras* come from?

The *maquila* system traces its origins back to 1964, when the U.S. Congress unilaterally cancelled the *bracero* program. This agreement had permitted Mexican farmworkers, nearly all men, to work in the United States as field hands. When some 200,000 *braceros* returned to Mexico without jobs, a major relief valve was lost to the Mexican government, whose approach to economic development has forced large numbers of peasants out of the countryside but has not provided adequate urban employment.

As early as the mid-1960s, some U.S. firms were already entering into informal agreements with Mexican entrepreneurs, opening factories across the border without the sanction of either government. In 1965, Mexico's minister of industry and commerce, Octaviano Campos Salas, toured Asia's export processing zones and returned a convert to this new approach to development. By 1970, the Mexican government had codified its Border Industrialization Program, offering incentives to foreign investors that were not available to national industry. Although most accounts credit the Mexican government with launching the *maquilas*, in fact the government was merely climbing aboard a trend that had already begun.

Have the *maquilas* lived up to the expectations with which they were introduced?

In both countries, the *maquilas* were introduced with promises that have failed to materialize. In Mexico, the plants were originally touted as a replacement for the *bracero* program. Yet from their inception they have never offered employment to people like the former *braceros*. Instead, they have targeted young, single women—bringing a new group of workers into the paid labor force. Meanwhile, the original unemployment problem has never been solved. One study in Juárez found that 75 percent of the men sharing a household with *maquila* workers—their fathers, husbands, brothers, etc.—were unemployed or underemployed, working as street vendors, day laborers, and the like.

In the United States, the *maquilas* were promoted as "twin plants," plants that would bring new jobs to both sides of the border. In fact, though, say union activists in border states, the U.S. "twin" usually amounts to a warehouse with only a handful of jobs. Production is concentrated on the other side of the border, where workers earn less than 8 percent of the wages paid to their U.S. counterparts.

How do government policies favor the *maquiladoras*?

Both countries support the *maquila* system through special provisions in their tariff codes. The Mexican government permits the temporary duty-free importation of equipment and raw materials, provided that 100 percent of the products are exported. Since there is no requirement that goods return to their country of origin, some firms, especially in electronics, import components from Asia, process them in Mexico, and market the finished products in the United States.

On the U.S. side, article 807 of the tariff code says that goods assembled abroad out of U.S. components may be reimported for sale, with duty paid only on the "value added" during assembly. This value added is assessed on the basis of the low foreign wage rates, rather than the market value of the products, which keeps tariffs down and makes the export of jobs economically attractive to U.S.-based corporations.

Will the number of *maquiladoras* continue to grow?

Every indication is that the *maquiladora* economy will keep growing. By 1986, *maquilas* had outpaced tourism as Mexico's second largest source of foreign exchange, surpassed only by oil. At that time, one out of every ten industrial workers was employed by the *maquilas*, and the percentage has continued to rise. Now, the automobile industry is joining electronics assembly (which has accounted for 60 percent of such plants), garment shops, and other light manufacturing firms in the *maquila* system. *Maquila* products, which made up only 10 percent of U.S. imports under the 807 program in 1970, now account for fully half.

In 1986, the Mexican government changed the law governing the plants so that they are permitted throughout the country, not just in the border zone. Recently, such major transnationals as Ford Motor Company, IBM, and Nissan, among others, have made large new investments. Investors from Japan and other countries are interested in the *maquilas* because of their low wage rates and easy access to U.S. markets. By the end of 1986, however, the *maquila* sector was still more than 90 percent U.S.-owned.

Women assemble tape cassettes in a Tijuana maquiladora.

GARY MASSONI

A CRISIS OF DEVELOPMENT

Where did Mexico's economic crisis come from?

The fortunes of the *maquiladora* system are intimately tied to Mexico's overall economic situation. Since the 1940s, Mexico's industrialization policies brought high rates of economic growth—averaging 6.7 percent a year. However, many workers and peasants were left out of the country's growing prosperity.

Eventually, the contradictions in this model began to unravel. Throughout the 1970s, transnational banks were eagerly promoting huge international loans. Mexico became the developing world's second largest debtor (see chapter 1 for more on the origins of the global debt crisis). Development plans relied on Mexico's extensive oil reserves, discovered in 1976, to repay the debt and finance the country's continued industrialization. Beginning in 1981, however, the bottom fell out of the oil market. Meanwhile, U.S. interest rates—which determine the amount of Mexico's debt-service payments—continued to rise.

With its back to the wall, the government continued to take out billions in new loans to pay the interest on the existing debt.

Currently, Mexico's foreign debt stands at more than $112 billion. In return for continuing credit, the International Monetary Fund (IMF) has demanded that Mexico devalue its currency and accept an economic austerity plan. In 1982, the value of the peso fell from 25 to the dollar to 150. Since another major devaluation in 1985, its value has continued to plummet. In early 1989, the peso stood at 2300 to the dollar, and the end was nowhere in sight.

What is the impact of the crisis on Mexican workers?

The IMF's austerity plan lays the burden of Mexico's crisis on poor working people. Government programs have been cut and subsidies for basic foodstuffs have been reduced or eliminated. The country's resources are channeled into debt payments rather than human needs.

For Mexicans, the consequences of this crisis have been devastating. In 1986 alone, purchasing power declined by more than half. In that single year, a million workers lost their jobs, raising the official unemployment rate to 17 percent. At least half of the workforce is underemployed. By 1987, real wages had fallen to their 1939 levels. Even government figures showed that 50 percent of the population did not have enough to eat. In 1987, inflation topped 140 percent. More than forty years of development were wiped out by five years of economic crisis.

Does anyone benefit from Mexico's hardships?

The crisis for working people offers many attractive features to the rich—both transnational corporations and traditional economic elites. As the peso shrinks, *maquila* wages cost less for U.S. firms. A Mexican worker's daily pay cost the U.S. employer about $10 in 1982, but only $3 in 1987. The crisis notwithstanding, Mexico's rate of return on investment, 18.3 percent, remains the highest in the hemisphere. In 1986, transnationals in Mexico paid out more than $440 million to their parent firms. Only $185 million of this sum was reinvested in Mexico; the rest was taken out of the country.

Wealthy Mexicans, meanwhile, sent more than $55 billion in assets to the United States

Matamoros, 1989: Distorted development means that maquila workers and their families lack basic services such as running water or electricity. Women must carry every gallon of water they use for washing dishes or clothes.

PEGGY FOGARTY/AFSC

between 1975 and 1985, hoping to protect themselves from the weakening peso by converting their assets to dollars. According to a study by the Morgan Guaranty Trust, if this capital flight had not occurred, Mexico would have only had to borrow $12 billion instead of the $112 billion it now owes to foreign banks.

THE CRISIS REBOUNDS

What is the effect of the Mexican crisis on U.S. working people?

In the United States, while some firms prosper because of Mexico's economic crisis, other elements in society lose out. The crisis has meant a drastic reduction of imports from the United States because of the shrinkage of the Mexican internal market as workers are less able to purchase goods. And, with interest payments eating up its foreign exchange, Mexico no longer has as many dollars to pay for U.S. products. Until recently, the United States always had a trade surplus with Mexico, but in 1985 there was a $5.8-billion trade deficit.

As Mexico imports less from the United States, more U.S. workers and farmers lose their jobs. This is added to the numbers of U.S. jobs lost directly to the *maquilas*.

What other factors link people in the United States and Mexico?

The economies of Mexico and the United States are profoundly interdependent. For Mexico, the United States is its largest trading partner for both imports and exports. For the United States, Mexico is the third largest supplier of imports and the fourth largest market for exports. Transnational corporations will continue to profit as Mexico's crisis deepens. Likewise, U.S. working people would benefit if Mexico's standard of living rose—because then Mexicans could afford to buy more U.S. products and because they would be less vulnerable as a cheap labor pool.

The intermingling of our two nations goes far beyond economics. Twelve million U.S. citizens are of Mexican descent. In addition, millions of other Mexicans have crossed the border as undocumented immigrants. The entire U.S. Southwest was part of Mexico until it was seized by the United States by military force between 1835 and 1853.

Nonetheless, the realities of Mexican society and culture are all but invisible in the United States. When we do see images of Mexico, they are generally rife with inflammatory and racist stereotypes about undocumented workers—who are blamed for unemployment—and drug smugglers—who are blamed for the U.S. drug problem. Almost

PEGGY FOGARTY/AFSC

The view from Matamoros: trucks line up on the U.S. side of the border, ready to transport maquila products to the U.S. market. The river in the foreground is the Rio Bravo (Rio Grande), which marks the Mexico-U.S. border.

never do we have an opportunity to hear from ordinary people in Mexico about their problems and what they think the solutions might be. It is long past time for working people on both sides of the border to explore our common interests through increased communication, exchanges among unions and other organizations, and solidarity.

ACTIVISM IN THE MAQUILADORAS

What issues are *maquila* workers most concerned about?

Most of the issues raised by *maquila* activists have to do with working conditions. According to U.S. trade unionists, when U.S. plants move to Mexico, the speed of production is routinely increased by 25 percent. After four or five years, many women can no longer stand the pace, and they are forced to leave *maquila* work. Often, their only alternative is to work in the "informal sector" of the economy—taking in laundry, selling snacks in the street, and the like.

Everywhere, health and safety is a matter of paramount concern. Gloria, who works for Kemet (Union Carbide) in Matamoros, a town at the eastern tip of the Mexico-Texas border, has been active for years in trying to improve health conditions in the plants. Following a 1988 trip to investigate *maquila* conditions in various towns, Gloria had this story to tell:

> In Ciudad Juárez we met a young man who told us he works with radioactive materials. The company, which manufactures smoke detectors, has told him that the radioactivity is minimal and that all he needs to do is use a small protector. This is an apparatus like a bracelet that is connected to a line over his head. As long as he wears this bracelet on his wrist, they told him, he will be completely safe. We made him see that they were lying to him. We told him of the risks he was running and he was very surprised.

At Kemet, years of efforts by activist workers have won significant improvements in safety conditions. Gloria recounts:

> Before, we had to put our bare hands right in the water with the components to brush off the degreasers. Now we have glove boxes, where we put our hands into the gloves and use tongs, so that we never have to touch the methylene chloride. Everything is pumped in through pipes and the components are washed under pressure. The used methylene chloride is

stored in tanks and returned to the United States for disposal.

In the past, says Gloria, "after so many years of putting their hands in that liquid, the workers had an infinity of health problems." In the United States, methylene chloride is regulated as a known carcinogen, but such hazards are routinely concealed from *maquiladora* workers. Now, some Mexican workers' groups are turning to U.S. unions for assistance in obtaining vital health and safety information.

One reason things have changed at Kemet is that the workers sought the support of the United Church of Christ, which owns stock in Union Carbide, the parent firm. After church representatives communicated their concerns to corporate officials in New York, safety practices at Kemet changed dramatically. As this story illustrates, the threat of public exposure is an important tactic in demanding corporate accountability. Other such efforts are described in chapter 5, which takes a detailed look at cross-border initiatives.

What is the environmental impact of so many high-technology plants?

Hazardous conditions inside the plants can leave behind lasting problems outside. One of the best-known cases is that of the Mallory children, a group of two dozen children in Matamoros who suffer from a common birth defect. Dr. Isabel de la O Alonso, head of the Matamoros School of Special Education, began to notice in the late 1970s that a series of these children were arriving in her school. They were mildly to profoundly retarded and shared a common appearance, "in some ways like that of children with Down's syndrome," the doctor says. "Their condition does not correspond to anything that has ever been described in medical literature. But clearly they are all the same."

In taking histories from parents, the school learned that all of the mothers had worked at a single *maquila*—Mallory Capacitors—during their pregnancies. While there, they were exposed to PCBs and other substances. Mallory left Matamoros in 1975 and its parent firm, P.R. Mallory, no longer exists, swallowed up in a series of corporate takeovers. "At this point," says Dr. de la O, "we see no possibility of seeking compensation." Recently, the U.S. Centers for Disease Control have taken an interest in the case.

An issue that is only beginning to surface is the disposal of toxic waste by *maquila* plants. According to a March 1988 expose in the *Austin American Statesman*, a Texas newspaper, only eleven out of 400 *maquilas* surveyed are returning their waste to the United States for proper disposal. Much of the rest is simply flushed down the drain or dumped in remote areas. The newspaper quoted a Mexican environmental engineer, Rene Franco, who charges that Mexico is being used as a "wastebasket" by the *maquiladora* industry.

Of course, once these wastes are in the environment, they won't stop at the border, points out Victor Muñoz, a Texas official of the AFL-CIO. Is *maquila* waste "contaminating our drinking water, our rivers, our air?," asks Muñoz. "For the benefit of all the working people of Texas we need the answers."

PEGGY FOGARTY/AFSC

How are women in the *maquiladoras* affected by sex discrimination?

Anthropologist Patricia Fernandez Kelly, who has written widely on the *maquiladoras*, observes that traditional attitudes persist that women are "supplementary" wage earners, even though *maquila* women supply vital income to their families and many are the heads of their households. Because of this "gender mythology," says Fernandez Kelly, "the fact that they are paid unusually low wages even for low-skilled occupations is not seen as a problem by government officials, legislators, and union leaders."

The organization of the *maquila* hierarchy makes occupational advancement a near-impossibility for women. Technical and supervisory positions are filled almost entirely by men. When technical personnel are needed, they are recruited from outside; production workers, who are mainly women, are almost never trained for such jobs.

Paternalism is another part of management's strategy to maintain control of the *maquila* workforce. At Dimit, reports Luisa, colored lollipops are strung over the work-

ers' heads to signify the quality of their output: green for good, blue for poor, orange for very poor. Fernandez Kelly quotes the superintendent of a major electronics plant in Ciudad Juárez:

> We like to hire girls who don't have too much experience because they aren't spoiled. We shape them to our needs by appealing to their feminine sensibilities. Then you can trust they won't fly off the handle, making unrealistic demands or joining unions. We like to think of our company as a family where everyone knows their duties.

Ironically, in some areas, such as Ciudad Juárez, *maquila* employers cannot find enough women to fill jobs and so increasing numbers of very young men are being hired into the plants. The reason for this seeming labor shortage reveals a lot about Mexico's desperate economic straits. With the value of their wages slashed by repeated devaluations of the peso, many women can no longer afford to work in the *maquiladoras*, especially those with families to support. Instead, they are choosing to slip across the border to seek jobs as maids or factory workers on the U.S. side. To make the crossing, they risk rapes, beatings, and deportation—for wages that may be as low as $40 a week.

What is the role of labor unions in the *maquiladoras*?

Only a small minority of *maquiladoras*— perhaps as few as 10 percent—are unionized. In Tijuana, Mexicali, Nogales, and Ciudad Juárez, where most *maquiladoras* are lo-

Young maquila workers study a handbook detailing their legal labor rights as their mother looks on. Informal sessions like these are a keystone of labor organizing in the maquiladoras.

Workers earn 55 cents an hour assembling lock cylinders at this maquiladora in Nogales, Sonora, which borders Nogales, Arizona.

cated, there are few if any unions. Where unions do exist, some are independently organized by the workers but many are established by the companies themselves.

In some cities near the eastern end of the border, however, such as Matamoros, Reynosa, and Piedras Negras, the majority of the *maquiladoras* are unionized. Nearly all of these unions are affiliated with the CTM (Confederation of Mexican Workers or Confederación de Trabajadores Mexicanos), the country's largest labor confederation. The CTM in its turn is a mainstay of the PRI, the political party that has dominated Mexico's government for more than fifty years.

In many border cities, the CTM leaders are men who are also large landowners and wield great economic and political power. The CTM generally supports the growth of the *maquiladora* program and cooperates with local officials and manufacturers to maintain a labor climate that will be attractive to investors.

Increasing union democracy and the responsiveness of the CTM to the needs of the rank and file are top priorities for activists among the *maquila* workers. In many cases, once workers are organized around a particular demand, union officials will back them up. In a few places, especially Reynosa, sustained efforts for a more open union have led to the entry of rank-and-file workers into union office.

What is the scope of labor activism in the *maquiladoras?*

Because the CTM has been slow to follow the lead of the rank and file, much of the labor activism in the *maquiladoras* is carried out by informal workers' groups operating outside of any institutional structure. The experiences of Roberto, the young garment worker whose comments opened this chapter, are typical.

At the time he made the observations quoted earlier, Roberto had recently been fired from Vestamex, a large garment factory, for organizing activities. Vestamex and an adjacent plant, Camisas de Juárez, are owned by Fashion Industries of Florida, which sells high-quality garments to Farah, Levi's, and other firms. Angered by what Roberto described as "an incredible speedup," workers began meeting outside the factory to discuss what action they should take:

Soon as many as fifty people were attending the meetings. We were well along in our plans for a work stoppage and were working on our list of demands when somebody told the company what we were planning. One morning at 9:00, the company's security guards arrested two of us and locked them in the office. Then everybody—1200 workers in both plants—stopped working. We occupied the factory and would not leave. They had to let our friends go. Eventually we won nearly all our demands: a 10 percent raise, transport subsidies, payment of our [legally mandated] benefits.

Because of the movement, fifty of us were fired, so that became another struggle. Only ten wanted to return to their jobs. The rest of us knew all the ways the company can get back at you after something like that. All we wanted was our severance pay, and we got that.

One of the demands at Vestamex was for registration of an independent union. At three-way negotiations between the workers, management, and local labor authorities, an agreement was signed that included such a provision. Once the strike was over, however, the workers were informed that they were already represented by a union. "We had never heard of this union," said Roberto, "never seen it." Nonetheless, labor authorities at the local and state level maintained that they could not grant a new registration with a union already in place. At the time he gave the interview quoted above, Roberto said the workers were planning to appeal to the national labor board in Mexico City. Prospects for a reversal, however, were remote.

Reynosa. An important moment in *maquila* labor history came in 1983-84, when a wildcat strike began at a Zenith plant in Reynosa. Ultimately, 12,000 workers at nine plants were involved in what became the first general strike in the *maquilas*. Scenes from this strike are shown in the film *The Global Assembly Line*. Originally called to demand a wage increase, the strike grew to embrace other issues, including corruption in the management of the transport system most workers relied on and calls for a change in CTM leadership.

After a complicated struggle, a greatly expanded union leadership was chosen by the membership in free elections and a new union head was sent from Mexico City. Many of the workers involved in the initial strike now hold office in the union. Today, workers in the *maquiladoras* know when their contracts expire, who negotiates them, and what the role of a union should be. Women have taken a leadership role in some plants, participating in contract negotiations, union meetings, and other union affairs. Women workers also played a major role in acquiring houses for workers through a government housing program.

Despite threats made throughout the strike, Zenith and the other *maquiladoras* have not left Reynosa. The plant where the strike began has actually expanded its operation, and Zenith recently established a new *maquiladora* in Ciudad Juárez.

Other labor gains. Most labor disputes in the *maquiladoras* are less spectacular, centering on demands for small, concrete improvements in working conditions. Informal groups often meet outside the workplace to discuss their problems and study their rights under Mexico's labor code. Through such mutual support they are emboldened to make demands on management and call on the CTM to back them up.

The story of Carmen, the ECC worker quoted earlier, illustrates the flavor of the new activism in the *maquiladoras*:

One time we had a wildcat strike. In a certain area of our plant, the lights were so bright they hurt our eyes. Then management changed the work process, introducing chemicals and solvents in an area that had never had them before. The change was very noticeable. People were suffering from eye irritations. At last three workers walked off the line and the others followed. This was after we had spoken to the supervisor, the delegate, the superintendent, and finally the union. We had taken all these steps with no results.

After the wildcat, management made changes in response to our complaints but they fired the three workers who had started it. So those three threatened a lawsuit, if the company did not give them their legal severance benefits. Finally they all got their severance. These advances have taught management to respect us. When new managers come in they are confronted by the workers and they too learn respect.

Through such tactics, workers in various plants have fought successfully to obtain improved safety equipment such as gloves or eyeglasses. Individual extractors have been installed to remove fumes from work stations where soldering is performed. In other cases, women have spoken out against sexual harassment by supervisors or have successfully protested arbitrary firings and disciplinary actions.

A frequent focus of worker activism is the *comisiones mixtas*, or joint commissions, legally mandated bodies with representatives from management, the union, and the rank and file that are supposed to monitor workplace health and safety. In the past, these commissions existed only on paper;

today, they are playing an active role in more and more plants. Following the lead of the rank and file, the CTM is also putting more emphasis on the *comisiones mixtas*.

What are some of the longer-term strategies under consideration in the *maquiladoras?*

As we have described, although labor activism is on the upswing in the *maquilas*, so far very little of it has taken a clear organizational form. This results from a variety of factors, including the sometimes equivocal role of the CTM. Another problem is the extreme isolation of most border communities. Workers have few allies to turn to and are extremely vulnerable to threats of blacklisting or violent intimidation, both of which are far from rare.

At this writing, some of the informal women's groups based in the eastern end of the border are preparing to open an *asociación civil*, the Mexican equivalent of a nonprofit corporation, that would serve as an educational and support center for *maquila* workers. Such an organization could greatly increase the ability of these groups to coordinate outreach to workers and organize public campaigns while minimizing the threat of reprisals.

Various strategies are under discussion for broader public campaigns around the *maquilas*. More than once, *maquila* plants have shut down and left the country without paying the required severance benefits. When one such shutdown occurred in Ciudad Juárez, a resulting hunger strike by former employees forced industrial promoters and city officials to contribute more than seven million pesos to satisfy the workers' claim. While it was the company's legal obligation to pay the workers, the city's leaders did so in order to maintain the reputation of the *maquila* industry. Currently, some groups are pressuring the government to require *maquiladoras* to post a bond to protect the

workers' interests if the plant should shut down.

Other groups have proposed a campaign around *utilidades'* or profit sharing. Under Mexican law, companies are legally required to distribute 10 percent of their profits among employees. However, the Mexican government permits the *maquiladoras* to set up their accounts so that they show no profit—all of the profits are concentrated in the parent firm in the United States. In one recent year, a Zenith plant paid its workers *utilidades* equivalent to $1.20 apiece. In contrast, workers from a Mexican-owned chemical plant in the border region received the equivalent of $2000 to $4000.

Union affiliation and the role of the CTM are highly controversial throughout Mexico's labor movement, and on these issues the *maquila* activists have no single direction. Some favor the formation of independent unions. Others feel that because the institutional power of the CTM is so great, pressuring it to become more responsive is the best strategy.

Whatever concrete strategies emerge, however, signs are that an irreversible process is taking place at the border. Workers are experiencing the power of collective action. Women, still a large majority of the *maquila* workforce, are also learning a new self-respect and independence of thought and action. These are the words of Clara, a Zenith worker in Reynosa who became shift representative for her plant as a result of the 1984 strike:

> Before, I was silent. I might listen and take notes, but I could not talk. Even when they asked my opinion I would not say anything. No one ever knew who I was. But then I went to some meetings [where] I had to speak up. And I found that the more I talked, the more people liked it. I couldn't believe it. This is how it starts: you begin to look at your own problems and it wakes you up so that no one can make you turn back.

REACHING ACROSS THE BORDER

As the *maquila* system grows, increasing numbers of U.S. groups, including local unions, church and community organizations, women's groups, and the top leader-

ship of the AFL-CIO are beginning to take an interest. In communities on both sides of the border, a variety of activists, health professionals, and others are responding to the *maquila* workers' requests for support and information sharing.

Many types of actions are being undertaken. One approach is putting pressure on Congress to restrict or repeal the tariff breaks granted to the *maquilas*' parent companies in the United States. Other groups are focusing on public outreach and education. Workshops on workplace chemical hazards have been given by U.S. union staff to Mexican workers. Efforts to build cross-border solidarity are described in chapter 5.

A Note on Sources

Information in this chapter is drawn from the files of AFSC's Maquila Project, from an unpublished presentation by Maria Patricia Fernandez Kelly, and from interviews with U.S. and Mexican workers. Published sources include "Mexico: Whose Crisis, Whose Future?", *NACLA Report on the Americas,* XXI:5-6, December 1987; and "The United States and Mexico: Face to Face with New Technology," Policy Perspective No. 8 from the Overseas Development Council.

PEGGY FOGARTY/AFSC

What does the future hold for this young Mexican? Will she work in the maquiladoras like so many of her older sisters?

4. After Marcos: Labor in the Philippines

In 1979, Elfreda Castellano joined Dynetics, Inc., a semiconductor firm. In a stuffy room emanating with fumes, she rinsed circuits in acids from 10:00 at night to 8:00 in the morning. Then she started getting sick. At first [she suffered] severe headaches, nosebleeds, and colds. By 1981 she developed skin rashes and bruises on her legs. Her application for job transfer was denied; at that time her quota was 22,000 circuits a day. Nor was she given any medical benefits by management. After three years on this job, her rashes spread and ruptured; nodules appeared in her groin. Freda died in 1982. Her illness was diagnosed as cancer of the lymph nodes.

This is just one of the stories collected in *Tales of the Filipino Working Women*, a booklet compiled by the Committee for Asian Women. In capsule form, it illustrates many of the problems the global factory has brought to the Philippines. Here is another story, this one excerpted from *Voices of Women Workers*, published by the Philippine Resource Center in Berkeley:

We are aware of management's various ways of trifling with women, both single and married. Sex exploitation is made easy through the appraisal system which is done every six months. It is when promotions, salary increases, demotions, transfers to other departments or firing[s] are conducted. If an appraiser happens to "like you" and you won't accept his invitation for a date, he can rate you lower than your actual performance. Many women are left with no choice but to accept the dates.

Both of these stories are from the waning years of the dictatorship of Ferdinand Marcos, who fell from power in February 1986 in a military uprising backed by massive civilian support. The fall of Marcos and his replacement by Corazon Aquino raised hopes that a more democratic government and the possibility of some real reforms had come to the Philippines.

Within a year or two, however, those hopes had vanished. Many Filipinos now say that poverty and government violence in their nation are worse than ever. Vigilante groups—similar to the death squads of Central America—are branding anyone who dares to speak out as "subversive" and murdering civilians with impunity. In the export processing zones that house foreign corporations, conditions have not improved at all. The working conditions described above, coupled with low wages and violent repression of strikes and union organizing drives, have prompted many Filipinos to join their country's labor movement.

Although the U.S. media are generally silent about the Philippines, it is a country of great importance for those in the United States who are concerned about the global factory. Transnational corporations, a majority of them headquartered in the United States, dominate the Philippine economy. U.S. military installations there—Clark Air Force Base and the naval base at Subic Bay—are the largest bases in the world outside U.S. territory, and the backbone of U.S. forces in the Pacific.

These bases do not only serve as a permanent reminder of the threat of U.S. military intervention. They have also generated an enormous "hospitality" or prostitution industry, with thousands of women forced to turn to sex work once they are laid off from jobs in the export processing zones. All of these issues will be in the public spotlight in 1992, when the lease for the U.S. bases is up for renegotiation.

The labor movement, other social movements, and a growing guerrilla rebellion are all pressing demands for basic change in the Philippines. As these political pressures mount, the Philippines is becoming a major arena for "covert" U.S. military intervention. Nowhere in the world is the connection more apparent between the global factory and the growing threat of all-out war.

This chapter will explore the situation of Philippine labor, focusing on women, who make up 80 percent of the workforce in the export processing zones. We will also take a look at what has happened in the Philippines since the 1986 change in government.

LOSING LABOR'S SUPPORT

What was Aquino's initial stance on labor issues?

On May 1, 1986, a scant three months after assuming power, Corazon Aquino addressed a half million wildly cheering Filipino workers at the traditional May Day celebration in Manila's Rizal Park. These were the people who had massed in the streets during the nonviolent uprising that finally toppled the Marcos dictatorship. They supported Aquino in the presidential election campaign that preceded the uprising because of promises that she now repeated in her May Day speech. Filipino workers, she said,

are broken victims of the avarice of individuals and of an oppressive social structure and hostile labor laws. . . [W]henever workers seek to organize and press for legitimate demands, they are subjected to harassment, intimidation, and violent dispersal by goons, by the police, or by the military. Union busting is a common occurrence and oftentimes happens with the direct participation of the government agencies which are supposed to protect workers. . . . I pledge to work for the repeal of repressive laws and for the dismantling of economic structures that keep workers in a state of quasi-slavery.

Today, many workers regard Aquino as no different than Marcos. "Before we thought of her as our Auntie Cory," says a 32-year-old mine worker, Pablo Pinengeo. "We trusted her, but no more. She promised to help the workers, but nothing is changed."

What caused the turnaround in Aquino's labor support?

In the first months of the new government, unions heeded Aquino's call for maximum restraint in labor demands. They even offered to mobilize defense for her government against threats of a coup by rightwing military elements. But a series of events soon disillusioned them.

On November 13, 1986, Rolando Olalia, the 52-year-old chairman of the progressive labor federation Kilusang Mayo Uno (KMU, or May First Movement), was murdered together with his driver. Olalia had also been chosen to head the newly organized Partido ng Bayan, the People's Party.

Most observers assumed—as the still unconcluded official investigation demonstrates—that Olalia's assassination was the doing of the rightist faction in the government, made up primarily of unreformed military officers. This faction was strongly opposed to any government cooperation with the "cause-oriented" or popular organizations. It criticized Aquino for "coddling communists."

The rightists struck again two months later—this time openly—when government troops fired on a peaceful demonstration for land reform on January 22, 1987, attended by 10,000 peasants and workers. Eighteen people were killed in the Mendiola Massacre, as it was known. In both cases, despite some expressions of remorse, Aquino did little to bring those responsible to justice.

Nor did she heed popular clamor to crack down on these remnants of the Marcos dictatorship, which were also destabilizing

Since the days of the Marcos dictatorship, the labor movement has been one of the most powerful organized forces in the Philippines in fighting for social justice. The photo below depicts a 1984 general strike in Davao City that blocked all the highways leading into the area.

CCHRP

her government by successive coup attempts. Instead, she continued to woo the military, turning a blind eye to their repression of labor and progressive groups. As one well-informed western diplomat remarked, "She's more interested in making sure the military is solidly on her side."

Also in January 1987, soon after another failed military coup, Aquino fired her minister of labor, Augusto Sanchez. A human rights lawyer who had defended political prisoners during the Marcos years, Sanchez was strongly opposed by the military, big business, and foreign interests, who branded him "too pro-labor." Michael Armacost of the U.S. State Department commented, "I'm apprehensive that the labor minister is attacking multinationals [and] endorsing strikes. . . . They've got to rein Mr. Sanchez in or get him to change his policy views." To replace Sanchez as labor minister, the president appointed an official of the Employers Confederation of the Philippines.

How has labor legislation fared under the new government?

In February 1987, Aquino issued her long-awaited Executive Order 111, amending the Labor Code. To the disappointment of workers, the order failed to repeal the two most hated anti-labor laws of the Marcos regime. These were BP (Parliamentary Law) 130, which imposes serious restrictions on the right to strike, and BP 227, which in effect legalizes the hiring of strikebreakers. Commented current KMU chairman Crispin Beltran, "We were asking for the repeal of the repressive Marcos labor laws. What we got were morsels." Both laws were being applied with renewed vigor against striking workers.

FORCED OVERTIME

"At Semiconductor Devices of the Philippines, management forced us to work overtime by simply holding our time cards. Should we decide to leave the company premises without punching the time card, we would be marked absent and would not be paid for our day's work. If we insisted on having our time cards, management would issue warnings on us for not working overtime."

—Electronics worker, quoted in Tales of the Filipino Working Women

May Day 1987 brought yet another disappointment. Aquino announced a labor package that failed to include a salary increase. She also rejected union demands for integration of an emergency cost-of-living allowance into the basic daily wage of $1.70. Both benefits had previously been approved by a Tripartite Conference among labor, management, and government. Crispin Beltran declared the government action to be "an insult to the Filipino workers" and "a clear betrayal of [their] rights and welfare."

The final stroke came on October 20, 1987, when Aquino responded to a general strike staged by a broad labor coalition calling for an across-the-board daily wage increase of 50 cents. In a speech before 1000 local and foreign business figures, Aquino—to the lusty applause of her audience—castigated militant labor as "an unruly minority" abusing the right to strike. She went on to say, "I therefore order the police and other peacekeeping authorities to . . . remove all illegal blockades at the factory gates. A special peacekeeping force . . . is now being trained to enforce return-to-work orders . . . issued by the [Labor] Department."

Hours after her speech, the Manila police swept down on eleven strike-torn factories and broke the picket lines, with no prior clearance from the Labor Department. Other government agencies rushed to follow the president's lead. The cabinet discussed plans forbidding strikes in the export processing zones for a period of five years. The military threatened to use force to dismantle strike barricades and to arrest those who refused to obey anti-strike orders.

Workers, for their part, voiced concern that the president had "declared war" on progressive unionism and that they were now back in a state of "de facto martial law."

A SOCIETY IN REVOLT

What are the roots of the conflict in the Philippines?

The problems of the Philippines do not end with the labor movement. Virtually every sector of society is in growing turmoil. Centuries of grinding poverty under colonial rule have been followed in modern times by policies that favor profits for transnational corporations at the expense of human needs.

In the countryside, where 70 percent of Filipinos live, the guerrilla forces of the New People's Army (NPA) and other groups are a growing threat to government power.

During the 1970s and early 1980s, above-ground opposition to the government was at a low level, held in check for a while by the mass arrests and human rights abuses under martial law, which was instituted by Marcos in 1972. Then, in 1983, returning opposition

politician Benigno Aquino, husband to Cory, was gunned down at the airport by Marcos forces.

After his assassination, the aboveground movement exploded. Peasant organizations, human rights groups, the women's movement, the labor movement—all swelled tremendously in numbers and in defiance of government repression. For the first time, middle-class groups joined the opposition in massive numbers. For a while, they were joined by some of the traditional elite, who felt that Marcos was becoming more of a liability than an asset in the struggle to contain the popular movements and defeat the NPA.

This assessment was shared by many within the U.S. government, which was concerned not only for the stability of U.S.-based corporations but also for the security of its military bases in the Philippines. At U.S. urging, Marcos staged an election to shore up his legitimacy in February 1986.

Thrust into the limelight as Benigno's widow, Corazon Aquino became the opposition's candidate. When Marcos tried to steal the election from her, the people took to the streets and key figures in the military threw their support to Aquino. Seeing Marcos as completely isolated, the U.S. government also withdrew its support. With scarcely any bloodshed, the dictator had fallen.

What is the record of the new government on economic issues?

Swept into office on the shoulders of the popular movement, Aquino promised to make a break with the old ways, to meet the growing demands for economic reform, human rights, and social justice. The paragraphs that follow review how the government she heads has kept these promises.

Overall indicators. The central fact about the economic situation is that it has hardly changed. The Philippines remains one of the poorest and least developed nations in Asia, with 70 percent of families living below the poverty line and nearly half of the paid labor force either unemployed (11 percent) or underemployed (36 percent). It also suffers from a starkly inequitable income distribution, with the richest 10 percent of families controlling 37 percent of the total national income, while the poorest 30 percent scrimp by on 10 percent of the national income.

A 50-cent-a-day (10-peso) raise for industrial and agricultural workers—the key demand of the October 1987 general strike—was finally approved by the Philippine Congress in December 1987, after a campaign of more than a year. This increase brought the minimum daily wage up to $3.10 (64 pesos). If this figure is adjusted for the effects of inflation, the raise meant that real wages were restored to their 1984 level, still

Children of migrant sugar workers on the Philippine Island of Negros. The sugar workers union is one of the mainstays of the KMU.

15 percent lower than the 1981 level. Even with the increase, the minimum wage would cover only 62 percent of the estimated cost of living for a family of six.

Foreign debt. The Philippines is the seventh largest debtor nation in the world. The country's debt mushroomed from $2.21 billion in 1972, at the onset of martial law, to $26.25 billion by the end of 1985, the eve of Marcos's downfall. Two years later, the debt had grown to $28.4 billion, which the Aquino government has promised to repay down to the last penny.

In 1988, debt service alone—that is, payments on interest, not principal—topped $3 billion, swallowing up more than one third (37 percent) of the national budget and almost half (47 percent) of the country's export earnings. By 1989, debt service had risen to 44 percent of the budget. Programs to alleviate poverty will have to wait. Meanwhile, the government plans to continue borrowing. By the time Aquino's term of office expires in 1992, it is estimated that the debt will have climbed to $35 billion.

Trade and import policies. The Aquino government has followed the bidding of multilateral agencies like the World Bank and the International Monetary Fund to remove restrictions on trade, internally and internationally. It has removed price controls, and has even wanted to leave the minimum wage to free market play. It has removed licensing requirements for 1000 import items. In February 1988, Aquino vetoed a bill increasing the tariff on imported garments.

One result of such policies is that the market is flooded with cheap imports, which chokes fledgling national industries out of business. This, of course, translates to a further loss of jobs and has contributed to a deficit in the balance of trade that rose to $750 million in 1987—a 72 percent jump over 1986.

What is the role of foreign investment?

In the 1970s, Marcos opened up the economy to foreign investment. His generous concessions included tax waivers and unhampered repatriation of profits (that is, return of profits to the firm's home country). Marcos also promised a cheap and tamed labor force. From a total of $123 million in 1970, direct foreign investment in the Philippines skyrocketed to $2.05 *billion* in 1983—an incredible 1900 percent increase. U.S.-based corporations account for 54 percent of foreign investment, with Japanese firms a distant second at 15 percent.

In the Omnibus Investment Code of 1987, the Aquino government offered privileges to foreign investors that even Marcos had hesitated to grant. Transnational corporations were encouraged to go into every field of business, rather than limiting themselves to the export processing zones. A requirement that 70 percent of a company's equity or capital be Filipino was lowered to 60 percent, permitting 40 percent foreign ownership. Even this restriction can easily be waived to permit 100 percent foreign ownership. Transnational corporations are exempt from taxes that Filipino companies must pay. In the first four months of 1987, foreign investment registered a 225 percent increase over the same period in 1986.

What is the impact of all this foreign capital? First, economic independence is sacrificed. U.S.-based transnational corporations now have prominent holdings in strategic sectors like manufacturing, oil, banking and finance, chemicals, and electronics, giving them tremendous influence over the entire economy. Second, even more wealth is siphoned out of the country as corporate profits are repatriated. In 1986, the combined profit of 128 U.S.-based firms amounted to $200 million, or 58.5 percent of the total profits of the top 1000 corporations in the country.

With this degree of foreign control, a self-reliant economy and development that is geared to the needs of most Filipinos are out of the question. Further, the transnational corporations have a vested interest in keeping Filipinos poor, since the promise of

Manila, 1988: Corazon Aquino at the presidential palace.

CCHRP

cheap labor is the main reason they come to the Philippines. The TNCs—backed by the highly visible U.S. military—are a powerful ally for the Philippines' wealthy classes, which have strenuously opposed land reform and other development policies that address the needs of the impoverished majority.

Why is land reform a central issue?

In a basically agricultural society like the Philippines, landlessness is a central and explosive problem. Of a rural workforce of 10.2 million in 1985, only 1.5 million owned the land they were tilling, while 5 million were landless farmworkers, 2 million were tenant farmers, and 1.5 million were farming public lands. Even these figures are understated, because rural women and often entire families work in the fields alongside the men, but are not paid for their work or counted as part of the labor force.

Throughout the country, of the 5.7 million families below the poverty line, 3.8 million were from the peasantry. These impoverished families represented nearly two thirds of the rural population.

Transnational corporations dominate not only Philippine industry, but also agriculture. Eighty percent of the cultivated land is owned by agribusiness and a few traditional landlord families. For the Philippines' major crop, coconuts, 1 percent of the farms occupy 1.5 million hectares (3.7 million acres), half the land planted to the crop. In sugar, 12 percent of plantations cover 53 percent of all sugar lands.

Castle and Cooke (Dole), Del Monte, and other U.S.-based firms all have huge holdings. The workforce for transnational industries in the export processing zones, meanwhile, is largely drawn from the daughters of peasant families who can no longer survive on the land.

Land reform is the most basic foundation for real change in the Philippines. Aquino promised such a program during her election campaign. Soon, however, she was saying that "by sharing out land, you only create more problems." It was only in the wake of the Mendiola Massacre that Aquino came up with a land reform program. Even the World Bank has criticized her program as inadequate. And implementation of the plan has been left up to the newly elected Congress, 90 percent of whose members are big landowners. Aquino herself is of landlord stock; her family owns one of the country's biggest sugar plantations.

Meanwhile, even Aquino's timid moves have aroused the ire of traditional elites. Governor Daniel Lacson of the island of Negros told the president that sugar planters in his province are expanding their private armies and that "civil war might break out" if land reform is instituted.

Is government violence still a problem?

In human rights above all else, Aquino promised to be the antithesis of Marcos. Thus, it is here that a sense of betrayal is felt most keenly by those who supported her. Some say her human rights record is even worse than that of Marcos. Task Force Detainees, a prestigious human rights group, reports that between January and November of 1987 there were 208 cases of "salvaging," or assassination by death squads, 59 disappearances, 7170 political arrests, and 512 cases of torture of political prisoners. Most of the victims of such violations have been workers and peasants. Health workers. religious activists, human rights lawyers, and opponents of the U.S. military bases have also been targeted.

Militarization. Aquino promised to pursue a policy of "peace and reconciliation" combined with social reforms as a solution to 20 years of guerrilla insurgency. This policy, however, did not please the 300,000-strong military, which staged a series of coup attempts to underline its opposition to negotiations with the insurgents. With each attempt, the armed forces gained greater concessions.

Husking corn at a cooperatively owned farm in San Isidro, Kitapawan. The land for the farm was occupied by local peasants and taken over from an absentee landlord.

REBECCA RATCLIFF

In February 1987, after the collapse of peace negotiations with the National Democratic Front—the political grouping allied with the NPA—Aquino succumbed to military pressure, declaring that it was now "fighting time." In the words of one observer, she unleashed military operations of "unprecedented proportions which would make operations under the Marcos regime pale in comparison." As ever, counterinsurgency has entailed widespread violations of human rights for the civilian population.

The vigilantes. Perhaps the most alarming development under the Aquino administration has been the rise of the so-called vigilante groups. Personally endorsed by the president as civilian self-defense groups, they are actually paramilitary units. Most are organized by the military and draw their members from local hoodlums and fanatical religious sects.

In May 1987, an international fact-finding mission led by former U.S. Attorney General Ramsey Clark reported that these groups "have become notorious for harassing, torturing, and executing civilians." Their victims are invariably leaders or members of progressive trade unions, peasant organizations, Christian base communities, and others who are accused of sympathizing with communists. Such widespread terror was not seen even in the worst years of the Marcos regime.

What is the role of the United States?

The United States has been a dominant force in the Philippines since 1898, when it seized control of the country from Spain in the Spanish-American War. During the era of U.S. colonial rule, popular rebellions were suppressed more than once by U.S. military action. Although formal independence was granted in 1945, the United States has continued to dominate the country's economic and political life. As conflict deepens in the Philippines, U.S. intervention is intensifying. Aid to the Philippine military, for example, has increased from $88 million in 1986 to $125 million in 1989, with $200 million proposed for 1990.

Both remilitarization and the vigilante groups are seen in the Philippines as part of a U.S. counterinsurgency strategy of "total war at the grassroots level." All along, the U.S. government has urged a military solution to the Philippine conflict. When Aquino attempted to negotiate with the insurgents, the Pentagon attacked her efforts as a "forlorn hope" and stepped up aid to the Philippine military.

The rise of the vigilante groups followed increasing CIA activity in the Philippines and the entry of the U.S. ultra-right, led by Gen. John Singlaub of the World Anti-Communist League and CAUSA, the political arm of Sun Myung Moon's Unification Church. The Ramsey Clark mission linked the CIA to organizing the vigilantes and suggested that U.S. money was involved.

Summing up.

In the Philippines, economic and human rights issues are two sides of the same coin. The more the government turns its back on the demands of the poor, and the more it subordinates national needs to the requirements of transnational corporations, the more it must resort to repressive measures to remain in power, using its armed forces against its own people.

WORKER, WIFE, AND MOTHER

"I realized how difficult it was to be a worker and at the same time be a wife and a mother. Every day, I would start to wake up at 4:30 to prepare the breakfast and prepare the whole day's meals and food for the baby. After work, I would rush home before my mother left, to cook, wash, and clean the house. On weekend union meetings, I leave my baby with my mother. I believe that unions should start looking into child-care needs of our women workers. I am a bit lucky to have my mother attending to my child. Not all workers can have their mothers doing it for them."

—Filipina union activist, quoted in Women on the Global Assembly Line

SPOTLIGHT ON WOMEN WORKERS

What groups make up the women's movement in the Philippines?

With virtually every sector of Philippine society joining the national movement, women are no exception. More than fifty women's groups are joined together in a coalition known as Gabriela, whose member organizations represent women workers, peasant women, urban poor women, women from the middle class, women from health groups, women involved in daycare, women religious, and women from consumer associations. Gabriela sees its role as twofold: to mobilize women to join the national movement and to advocate women's particular concerns within that movement. Another group, Pilipina, works to improve the status of women through legislative advocacy, public education, and electoral politics.

In the Philippines, as in many Third World countries, feudalism, patriarchy, and foreign domination have long held women subservient. Traditional stereotypes have set the limits for women's participation in national development and the political process. Although a small women's movement began in the years before martial law, the fourteen years of the Marcos dictatorship politicized huge numbers of women. Women awoke to a consciousness of their potential for political participation and their need for economic and social emancipation.

The February 1986 uprising that swept Marcos from power dramatized that potential. Electronic media brought to the fore powerful images of unarmed women facing down tanks and soldiers, protecting ballot boxes in the face of guns and goons, and participating in protest actions in large and organized numbers.

How are women workers organized?

Women workers have banded together since 1984 in the Women Workers Movement, or the KMK (Kilusang ng Manggagawang Kababaihan), a member organization of Gabriela. With 30,000 members, the KMK is also a member of the KMU, or May First Movement, the progressive labor confederation. The KMK draws its membership from many different unions, and advocates for women's concerns within the labor movement and the larger national movement.

"The position of women in trade unions is changing," says KMK Secretary General Cleofe Zapanta. "Before, among union officers, the women were in the traditional positions of secretary and treasurer. But now there are lots of unions whose presidents are women. That's why we are training more women workers to be leaders."

The KMK addresses issues important to women workers, including nondiscrimination and equal opportunity in jobs, pay, and promotions; maternity leave and social services for working mothers; job security; and sexual harassment. With its focus on organizing previously unorganized women, the group continues to grow, drawing in new members from factories, plantations, stores, and offices.

Where unions already exist, says Cleofe Zapanta, "we try to have our demands

REBECCA RATCLIFF

included in the general union's demands. We see to it that the union officers understand our purpose. Because if you can't convince the union officers it is very hard to have the demands of women workers included. The KMU now has a Women's Commission for coordinating with us."

What is the overall position of women in the labor force?

Women face many types of discrimination in the Philippine economy. Although women constitute nearly 50 percent of the total population in the Philippines, they make up only 37 percent of the paid labor force. This figure, however, does not truly reflect their participation in work above and beyond their household tasks. In rural areas, where some two thirds of Filipina women live, they perform extensive unpaid farm work for their families, including backyard farming, help in seedbed preparation, marketing of farm produce, and the like. Domestic service, in which more than a million women are engaged, is regarded as "nonproductive" and not an occupation.

Of 7.2 million women in paid employment, more than a third (34 percent) are agricultural workers and about a fourth (24 percent) are sales workers. Thirteen percent are in service occupations, 12 percent (about 868,000) are industrial workers, and nearly 10 percent are in the professions (mostly teaching and nursing). Only 0.65 percent, or two for every ten male Filipinos, are at the management level.

Women's wages are generally less than two fifths of what men make in the same

Striking workers at Dimentranco, a ramie processing plant outside of Davao City. A majority of the plant's workers are women.

What is the situation of women industrial workers?

Women factory workers are concentrated in the garment, electronics, and food-processing industries. In electronics, out of a workforce of 38,700 in mid-1984, 85 percent were women, usually unmarried and between the ages of sixteen and twenty-five. As noted earlier, about 80 percent of workers in the export processing zones are women. The jobs for which they are hired require few skills and generally involve cleaning, assembly, and checking of minute parts. Employers claim to prefer women for their manual dexterity, meticulousness, patience with complex and monotonous work, and docility.

In industry, as everywhere, women are paid far less than men. Their average take-home pay is 292 pesos ($14.60) a week; they are often assigned work quotas that force them to work overtime. In one garment factory, which pays workers at a piece rate, the workers receive only 24 pesos ($1.20) a day instead of the minimum daily wage of 54 pesos ($2.70). A garment worker tells her story in these words:

> We work from 7:00 a.m. to 3:00 p.m. sewing pieces of jeans. Our quota is 400 pieces per worker for eight hours, but we are made to sew 250 more and we usually end up working fourteen hours. Most of us complain of ulcers, headaches, and kidney disorders due to fatigue and hunger. What makes us feel very exploited is the fact that we make jeans worth so many thousands of pesos and yet get 29 pesos ($1.80) a day only.

And from a pineapple cannery worker:

> Ninety percent of the workers in this cannery are women. Management claims women to be more diligent, easier to handle, and easier to fire. Thirty percent of the increase in profits comes from the labor power of the women compared to the 10 percent from the male workers. Why? Because women receive only half the pay of the male work force.

Factory women often work under conditions that are hazardous to their health. Workplaces are hot, stuffy, and poorly ventilated; noisy and poorly lighted. Especially in electronics factories, workers are exposed to radiation and toxic substances that can cause anemia and cancer.

REBECCA RATCLIFF

One of the Dimentranco strikers.

occupations. A 1986 census reported that the average monthly earning of female agricultural workers was 115 pesos ($5.75), compared to 1343 pesos ($67.15) for men. For industrial workers, the figures were 353 pesos ($17.65) for women, 2297 pesos ($118) for men; and for managers, 1676 pesos ($83.30) for women, 10,131 pesos ($506.50) for men.

What about women in agriculture?

Conditions are particularly harsh for the more than 2.4 million women who are paid agricultural workers. Their work includes planting, transplanting and weeding, harvesting, piling, and threshing—in addition to household tasks and child-rearing. In a typical plantation in Bicol, men receive starvation wages of 60 cents (12 pesos) a day, but women receive only 25 to 35 cents (5 to 7 pesos) a day.

Many women farmworkers leave for the cities after a short time, hoping to escape from poverty and find a better life. In the urban centers, they become a "marginal labor reserve" of disposable workers whose presence helps to keep wages down. Many of them end up as "hospitality girls," or prostitutes.

Most firms preferentially hire unmarried women, who are considered easier to handle and do not claim maternity benefits. In many factories, married women are encouraged to undergo sterilization by offers of incentives such as cash benefits and extended sick leave. Maternity benefits are often shortened and sometimes totally absent.

Sexual harassment is rife. Many times women are forced into sexual relationships with male supervisors or management in order to keep their jobs. Says one worker, "A single woman worker is likely to get the 'lay down or be laid off' treatment. We are called 'cheap bananas'."

Job insecurity is another serious problem. Factory jobs available to women rarely offer steady employment. Between 1981 and 1983, electronics and garments became the Philippines' top export earners, so jobs increased as the factories expanded to meet export demand. By late 1983, however, production had fallen nearly 17 percent in electronics, while employment in garment work had dropped 25 percent.

The downward trend continued through 1986 as factory after factory closed down in the Bataan Export Processing Zone. The fate of these women workers is tied to the ebb and flow of the distribution of work through-out the global factory—decisions in which workers do not take part in any country.

How are women workers responding to these conditions?

All of these problems have prompted women's growing involvement in labor activity. Often, once women become involved, they prove to be among the boldest and most effective organizers. In a historic general strike in the Bataan Export Processing Zone in 1982, workers directly challenged the Marcos regime's promise of a subservient labor force for transnational firms. Women workers provided the main force for the strike, and in fact were among the main organizers. This action was one of several developments that led to the founding of the KMK.

Many women activists in the Philippines are acutely aware of their place in the global factory, of the international economic restructuring that underlies their daily problems. They are exploring ways of making connections with potential friends and allies in the U.S. and other countries—particularly with people who are also grappling with the challenge of transnational corporate power. Some beginning efforts in that direction are described in chapter 5. Below, we conclude this chapter with a final look at the overall labor movement in the Philippines.

IF YOU CAN'T STAND THE HEAT . . .

"I was reassigned to the stitching cap operation. I had to stich 64 dozen in eight hours. Every day, I was bathed in my own sweat since there was no ventilation at all. We complained to the management, but they just said, "when you entered the company, you knew what was in store for you. If you cannot bear the heat, you can leave anytime you want. Each of you can easily be replaced by a hundred more." So we clung to what we had.

—Garment worker, quoted in Tales of the Filipino Working Women

LABOR STRUGGLES ON

What are the effects of the current government's labor policy?

As the Aquino government has grown increasingly estranged from workers, the military and the Labor Department have stepped up their repression of militant labor unions. Officers and organizers have been harassed and threatened, union offices are watched, and unions accused of being leftist are discriminated against by government services. Since the government's order to break up labor actions classified as illegal, the police and the military have been attacking picket lines and arbitrarily arresting labor leaders.

From the time Aquino assumed power in February 1986 up to August 1987, 263 workers were arrested in assaults on picketlines or similar incidents. During the same period, 46 workers were killed and another ten have disappeared—some in strikebreaking violence; others as victims of "salvaging." According to KMU Chairman Crispin Beltran, the KMU has lost about 25 percent of its membership because of government "covert and overt operations. They are relentlessly crushing militant unionism here."

What groups make up the Philippine labor movement?

As in many countries, the Philippine labor movement is divided between militant confederations, like the KMU, and "yellow" unions that are responsive mainly to government and business interests. The country's largest federation, with 1.3 million members, is the Trade Union Congress of the Philippines (TUCP), organized in 1975 as a labor

May Day march in Davao City, 1988.

Several smaller confederations have joined with the KMU to form the Labor Advisory and Consultative Council (LACC). This body, formed after the fall of Marcos, has taken a leading role in representing labor in the national tripartite conferences among labor, business, and government. It has also represented Philippine labor in conventions of the UN's International Labor Organization. It called the general strike of October 1987 and has been a leader in the fight for wage increases and the repeal of anti-labor laws.

What is labor's response to the political climate in the Philippines?

Despite the growing atmosphere of repression, labor activity is on the increase in the Philippines. Tempered by years of struggle during the Marcos dictatorship, the militant labor movement was not lulled into complacency by the apparent democratic opening in the first months of the Aquino administration. Between January and November 1987, 417 strikes were held, many against transnational corporations in the Bataan and Baguio Export Processing Zones and Nestle-Philippines, as well as the state-run National Steel Corporation.

The *welgang bayan* (people's, or general, strike) of August 26, 1987, called to oppose an oil price hike, paralyzed transportation in Manila and ten major cities throughout the country. The week-long industrial general strike of October 1987 affected 1166 firms all over the country and involved at least 600,000 workers. More can be expected, as labor pledges "to harness its vast human resources into a political force that could unite with other sectors and bring about the change we have long been fighting for."

center controlled by the Marcos government. It receives support from the Asian-American Free Labor Institute, a body sponsored by the AFL-CIO that has been linked to the CIA. Its former secretary general, Ernesto Herrera, now a member of the Philippine Senate on the Aquino slate, has called for even tighter labor laws, saying that labor leaders "who do not adhere to the national agenda of industrial peace [must] be arrested."

With 700,000 members, the KMU, founded in 1980, is already the second-largest labor center. Grouping together ten separate labor federations, it counts within its ranks the 40,000-member National Federation of Sugar Workers as well as the KMK. The KMU advocates both economic and political demands and has spearheaded most of the militant strikes and political demonstrations under both Marcos and Aquino. The group has been branded as a communist front by the military, and several of its leaders have become victims of right-wing death squads.

A Note on Sources

The text for this chapter was prepared by Chat Canlas while she was a Fellow of the Institute for Policy Studies in Washington, DC. Complete footnotes are available from AFSC's Women and Global Corporations Project.

5. Taking Action, Gathering Strength

Directly or indirectly, the global factory affects many millions of working people, in the United States and around the world. In preceding chapters, we have seen how the international movement of jobs is part of a complex system of interrelated developments. In the United States, the trend is toward the erosion of industrial jobs, a decline in union membership, and a falling standard of living for most people. In the Third World, its effects include distorted development, dramatic increases in poverty, and a snowballing economic crisis.

In response, many different kinds of groups have been seeking ways to place some limits on the tremendous power of transnational corporations (TNCs). In the United States, many such efforts have focused on plant closings, whether through collective bargaining, community/labor coalitions, or legislative campaigns. However, as we saw in chapter 2, these campaigns have mainly managed to ease the effects of plant-closings through severance benefits, retraining programs, and the like. With a few exceptions, they have not been able to affect the movement of industrial jobs from region to region or country to country.

As the plant-closings movement and labor movement grapple with questions of long-term strategy, many groups are placing increasing emphasis on reaching out internationally. For the TNCs, it is precisely the international mobility of production that characterizes the global factory. Attempts to challenge corporate power on a local or even a national basis are operating at a severe disadvantage. If a TNC faces unwelcome restrictions in one place, it can move on to another.

For a variety of reasons, the idea of building international networks is unfamiliar territory for many people in the United States. Because so many different groups are affected by the global factory, however, the potential coalition for such campaigns is enormous. Not only groups involved with domestic U.S. concerns but also those already seeking to reach out internationally could make common cause on these issues.

What groups would make up such a coalition? With union gains and unionized workplaces being targeted for attack, organized labor is an obvious actor. Many religiously based organizations also address the impact of economic dislocation on local communities. Both of these sectors already have extensive international ties. Unions, for example, relate to their counterparts in many parts of the world, through both established organizations and emerging solidarity networks. In recent years, U.S. labor networks concerned with Central America and South Africa have had a major impact on the overall labor movement. A newer network is in the early stages of building solidarity with Filipino workers.

Likewise, some religious bodies, concerned with poverty in the Third World, have come to appreciate how the global economic system works to maintain Third World "underdevelopment." And, even without a specific orientation toward labor issues, some groups that are working to oppose the U.S. role in southern Africa or Central America are also concerned with the role of TNCs in perpetuating unjust systems in those areas.

Outside of the organized labor movement, labor groups involved with nonunionized workers must often address the problem of TNCs. Since the impact of job loss is greatest for communities of color, organizations based in those communities also have a stake. The same is true for women's groups that focus on women's poverty, which is related in part to the declining availability of stable industrial jobs.

For workers and their communities, TNCs frequently pose serious problems of toxic waste and workplace exposure. Thus, groups concerned with workplace safety and health are another potential constituency, as is the environmental movement more generally.

A DEMOCRATIC RIGHT

"What has always been the case is now becoming apparent to more and more people as their futures are being destroyed— guiding the economy is a democratic right!"

—Tri-State Conference on Steel

As the Bhopal disaster demonstrated so graphically, toxic exposure is also an international problem.

Even some local and state governments, concerned with job creation and an eroding tax base, could lend their support. The same is true of some organizations concerned with economic development, both domestically and internationally. In particular, many groups concerned with integrating women into development programs have developed a thoroughgoing critique of the negative impact of TNCs on the status of women.

To what extent are these different groups actually beginning to work together? Where is coalition-building most fruitful? What are the most promising strategies? What are the obstacles in building a broadbased movement to address the global factory? To what extent does existing organizing address the needs of women and people of color? How effective are U.S. organizations in building ties with Third World workers' movements?

To explore these questions, we take a look at more than a dozen organizations in the United States. Each of the groups or campaigns described represents people who are affected by the international movement of jobs. Each is trying in some way to empower its constituency to stand up to the TNCs. All are grappling with the challenge of building international networks. Together, they offer a snapshot of the state of U.S. organizing around the global factory, taken as the decade of the 1990s begins.

DEINDUSTRIAL-IZATION

"Since 1979 more than 50 percent of all new jobs pay less than $7000 a year.
Meanwhile over 50% of West Coast shipbuilding has been lost. In a two-year period over 15,000 looms in the textile industry were lost—95 percent of them in Georgia, North Carolina, and South Carolina. In the past seven years 444 steel-related facilities have been closed. In the same period the famed Silicon Valley of California saw 16,000 people lose their jobs to plant closings."

—Tri-State Conference on Steel

EYES ON THE BORDER

The Case of Trico

Like hundreds of thousands of workers across the United States, employees of Buffalo's Trico Company learned in early 1986 that their jobs were moving south to join the *maquiladora* system on the Mexico-U.S. border. Trico, the world's largest manufacturer of windshield wipers, announced that it was laying off 1100 workers, keeping only 400 jobs at its Buffalo factory. The rest of Trico's jobs would move to "twin plants" in a pair of border communities, the Mexican city of Matamoros and Brownsville, Texas. Attrition had already reduced the workforce from its one-time high of 2500.

The move was necessary, said Trico management, because of foreign competition. Norm Harper, president of United Auto Workers (UAW) Local 2100, which represents Trico workers, disagreed. He issued a press statement arguing that Trico could remain profitable in Buffalo. The union had taken the lead in suggesting modernization plans as early as 1979, he reported—but management had never responded.

One of those concerned about the plant closure was Robert Beck, a local pastor in the United Church of Christ. "I was the cochair of an interracial task force," he explains, "and I knew that many of the layoffs would affect minorities." Beck invited Harper to address his group and explain why the move was unnecessary. Harper "was very persuasive," recalls Beck, and out of that meeting was born CRUCUL (pronounced *crucial*), the Coalition of Religious, University, Community, and Union Leaders.

In the two years and more since it was founded, CRUCUL has had a major impact, both on Buffalo and on awareness of the *maquila* issue nationally. Early on, Harper and Beck went on a fact-finding tour to Brownsville and Matamoros. They came back with videotapes and slides of their trip and spoke widely throughout the region about the realities of the *maquila* system. At the urging of CRUCUL members, several religious bodies in the region adopted resolutions on plant closures. The group's efforts have also helped to convince the UAW to take action on *maquilas* at the national level.

After repeated press conferences, CRUCUL attracted the attention of New York governor Mario Cuomo, who persuaded Trico management to agree to a joint labor/management study of how the threatened jobs might be kept in the state. The study found that Trico could save $36 million a year through modernization and joint problem-solving by labor and management. The union supported the study's suggestions, but Trico refused to adopt them.

Why would a firm refuse to make changes that would allow it to stay profitable in its present location? Some of CRUCUL's research may offer a clue. Several years back, according to a report in *Business First* magazine, Trico had purchased stock in both Ford and General Motors. Earnings from that portfolio were paid out as dividends of $6 million a year to Trico's stockholders, rather than being invested in modernization.

Meanwhile, according to a little-publicized federal law, if 30 percent of an automobile's components are manufactured abroad, the entire car is considered an import and thus is subject to looser safety regulations. "We believe one reason Trico insisted on moving to Mexico," says Robert Beck, "is so they could qualify Ford and General Motors cars to be considered as imports."

Concessions Without Commitments

On their fact-finding trip, Beck and Harper learned a lot more about the inner workings of the global factory. "At first," notes Harper, "people in Brownsville were resentful toward us—they wanted to know why we were against their having good jobs. But after they talked with us they realized that they too were losing out." According to Beck, "Trico said they would pay $4 an hour in Brownsville, but they're actually paying minimum wage. And this is for jobs that were skilled jobs in Buffalo. They're not paying any kind of health benefits—instead they're telling the workers to apply for food stamps and SSI [a form of public assistance]. So Trico is expecting the taxpayers to subsidize these jobs they're supposedly creating."

CRUCUL has also raised questions regarding the role of government, both local and federal, in promoting the move. The city of Brownsville donated city-owned land for the new Trico plant, charging a monthly rent of only 1.2 cents per square foot—a fraction of the market rate. But Trico has made no commitment as to how many Brownsville residents it will hire or for how long.

The federal government is also indirectly supporting the move. A quarter of Trico's new workforce is covered by a federal job-training program, which pays half their salary. Again, Trico has made no commitment as to how long these workers will keep their jobs once the training subsidy runs out. "We question why the federal government should subsidize them when they have abandoned skilled workers in Buffalo," comments Beck. "The company should have to pay for that itself."

Beck predicts that Trico will follow the common pattern of gradually reducing its operation on the U.S. side of the border to a thinly staffed warehouse and moving all

of the production jobs across to the Mexican plant. "In general," he notes, "after four years all of the jobs move from Texas to Mexico," according to statistics gathered by sociologist Tony Zeveletto at Southernmost University.

Beck and Harper were horrified by the conditions they found on the Mexican side of the border, including daily wages as low as $2.40. "I had to satisfy myself personally," says Beck, "that we weren't just taking a stand against Mexican workers. In fact, serious exploitation of Mexican women is going on. Women in the *maquiladoras* are working with piece-rate quotas that are 25 to 40 percent above the U.S. standard. After about four years, they lose their jobs because they can't keep up the pace—and then they are worse off than they were before. The plants are housed in these beautiful, windowless, air-conditioned buildings, but in terms of working conditions, they are sweatshops."

Despite all of CRUCUL's efforts, in December 1987, Trico began moving jobs to the border. The company's only concession was to keep some 300 jobs in Buffalo that had been going to move. An impact study sponsored by CRUCUL estimated that the shutdown will cost Buffalo as much as $126 million a year, including $100 million lost to the local economy, $15 million in increased welfare costs once unemployment runs out for the displaced workers, and $11 million lost in taxes.

CRUCUL, however, has continued organizing, shifting its energies to opposing government policies that foster the export of jobs. "As a union person," says Harper, "my focus is to stop the government from

Representatives of the Communications Workers of America traveled to Matamoros, Mexico in early 1989 to investigate the movement of jobs in their industry across the border.

Trash disposal is one of many basic services that is not provided for this Matamoros neighborhood where many maquila workers live. Even more serious, all along the border disposal of industrial wastes by the maquila companies themselves is virtually unmonitored.

using the taxpayers' money to support the demise of taxpayers' jobs.'' One successful effort came in late 1986, when the U.S. Commerce Department was forced to withdraw its sponsorship of an Acapulco trade show promoting *maquilas*. CRUCUL's story has also been widely reported in the media, in Europe as well as in the United States.

Currently, the group is one of many across the country fighting for plant closing legislation. Other legislative approaches are also being explored that could place some limits on the runaway growth of the *maquiladoras*. "We should be concerned," says Harper, "with elevating the living standards of Mexican workers up to ours—not lowering ours to the Mexican standard."

Pressure from Below

If not every community has given rise to a group as active as CRUCUL, the experience at Trico has been repeated again and again at countless plants in many different industries. Over the last decade, according to the AFL-CIO, U.S. firms have invested $2 billion in *maquiladora* plants, idling as many as 125,000 U.S. workers in the process. The pressure to take some action has mounted from workers at the local level to their national unions, and on up to the highest levels of the AFL-CIO.

An indication that this pressure is having an effect came in April 1988, when AFL-CIO leadership and presidents of several internationals met in Matamoros with Mexico's largest labor confederation, the Confederación de Trabajadores Mexicanos (CTM). From the U.S. side, the unions

represented included the UAW, the International Union of Electrical Workers (IUE), the International Brotherhood of Electrical Workers (IBEW), the International Ladies Garment Workers Union (ILGWU), the Amalgamated Clothing and Textile Workers Union (ACTWU), and others.

The two delegations agreed to form a binational committee on the *maquilas*, with representation from the four sectors most strongly affected—garments and textiles, the auto industry, electrical and electronics assembly, and ground transport. In addition to task forces in each of these industrial areas, regional task forces were formed to facilitate communication between unionists in bordering communities such as El Paso, Texas, and Ciudad Juárez; San Diego and Tijuana; and Brownsville and Matamoros.

So far, the garment/textiles task force has been the most active, according to Jeff Stansbury, the western states education director for the ILGWU. The group has held both U.S. and binational follow-up meetings. Joint education has been proposed, says Stansbury, on contracts, the structure of the industry, and health and safety issues.

"We have a lot to learn from the Mexicans," Stansbury notes, "and they can also benefit from the information we share. Both sides need thorough, up-to-date information on ownership patterns, products, capitalization, hiring policies, and connections between U.S. and Mexican plants. We also both need to know how garment firms are operating in export processing zones in other parts of the world. All of this information can flow directly into training and organizing efforts."

Who Speaks for Mexico?

Although such top-level contacts show that the issue is indeed being taken seriously, they also have some drawbacks. Chief among these is the policy of the AFL-CIO that it will work only through its official counterparts in other countries—in this case the CTM. Yet, as we described in chapter 3, only 10 percent of the *maquilas* have been unionized. Throughout the border area, the most vital and energetic labor organizing in the *maquilas* is taking place outside the CTM.

Some U.S. unionists say privately that changes inside Mexico may facilitate a more flexible approach to binational contacts. The CTM is an integral part of the Partido Revolucionario Institucional (PRI), which has held power in Mexico for more than 50 years. In the eyes of many observers, however, the elections of July 1988—in which the opposition had an unusually strong showing—were the beginning of the end for the monolithic nature of Mexican politics. Many observers believe that opposition candidate Cuauhtemoc Cardenas actually won the election, despite the official tally. As a result, a much broader range of voices within Mexico are demanding a say in national policy. In this new climate, there are greater opportunities for U.S. unions to talk to forces outside the CTM.

Beyond the AFL-CIO, U.S. unionists are more blunt about the limitations of working through the CTM. Amy Newell is secretary-treasurer of the United Electrical Workers union (UE), which is not part of the AFL-CIO. "Our staff have traveled to Juárez and Tijuana to meet with people organizing *maquila* workers," says Newell. "We have found that it is not really possible to establish union-to-union relationships because the official unions have surrendered the attempt to organize in the border area. Our connections are with smaller, progressive groups. We are in touch with them, we

List of Abbreviations

The list below explains the abbreviations used in this chapter.

ACTWU—Amalgamated Clothing and Textile Workers Union

AFL-CIO—American Federation of Labor/Congress of Industrial Organizations; U.S. trade union confederation.

AFSC—American Friends Service Committee

COSATU—Congress of South African Trade Unions; principal labor confederation in South Africa.

CRUCUL—Coalition of Religious, University, Community, and Union Leaders, Buffalo, NY

CTM—Confederación de Trabajadores Mexicanos (Confederation of Mexican Workers); largest trade union confederation in Mexico.

IBEW—International Brotherhood of Electrical Workers

ICFTU—International Confederation of Free Trade Unions

ILGWU—International Ladies Garment Workers Union

ILRWG—International Labor Rights Working Group, Washington, DC

IPS—Institute for Policy Studies

IUE—International Union of Electrical Workers

KMK—Kilusang ng Manggagawang Kababaihan (Women Workers' Movement); women's labor group in the Philippines.

KMU—Kilusang Mayo Uno (May First Movement); militant labor confederation in the Philippines.

LCAA—Labor Committee Against Apartheid, New York, NY

OTEP—Office Technology Education Project, Boston, MA

PRI—Partido Revolucionario Institucional (Institutional Revolutionary Party); dominant political party in Mexico.

PWSC—Philippine Workers Solidarity Committee

SCCOSH—Santa Clara Center on Occupational Safety and Health, Santa Clara County, CA.

SEIU—Service Employees International Union

TIE—Transnationals Information Exchange

TUCP—Trade Union Congress of the Philippines; official labor confederation in the Philippines.

UAW—United Auto Workers

UE—United Electrical Workers

UMW—United Mineworkers

UNTS—Unión de Trabajadores Salvadorenos (Union of Salvadoran Workers); nonaligned labor confederation in El Salvador.

WFTU—World Federation of Trade Unions

exchange information, but so far it's all fairly primitive— there's a lot more to do."

An important priority for UE is educating its 80,000 members about the realities of the global factory. "We do as much as we can," says Newell, "to combat the kind of jingoism that is promoted, sloganeering about 'buy American' and so on." A UE pamphlet on the topic is entitled *Corporate America's Biggest Export: Our Jobs*. "Much of the so-called foreign competition," the pamphlet notes, "isn't foreign at all. U.S.-based corporations are the single biggest cause of our trade deficit—and are the only exporters of U.S. jobs."

The UE approach differs from that of many other unions, which focus on foreign competition as the problem and often say little about the role of U.S.-based transnational corporations. UE also sponsors a sister union campaign and participates in a variety of legislative coalitions.

Organizing Binational Support

Some religiously based organizations have also chosen to operate more informally. The American Friends Service Committee (AFSC), a Quaker service organization, instituted its Mexico-U.S. Border Program in 1978. "Our staff became aware of the tremendous problems that *maquiladoras* were causing for Mexico," notes AFSC's Elizabeth Baumann. "At that time *maquilas* were not well-understood in the United States." Baumann is director of AFSC's *Maquila* Project.

At the border, AFSC coordinates its efforts with the Comité de Apoyo (Support Committee), a binational group in the Brownsville/Matamoros area involving health professionals and religious and community leaders. Through workshops, training programs, and informal networking, the group helps activists inside the *maquiladoras* increase their contacts with the outside world.

Through the Comité de Apoyo, U.S. trade unionists have been able to make direct contact with rank-and-file *maquila* workers, enabling them to learn first-hand about the realities of the border economy. Such communication has also been valuable to the Mexicans, providing them with access to important information. Examples include details of U.S. union contracts and safety materials about toxic substances they may encounter in their workplaces.

AFSC has also undertaken public education about the *maquila* system, providing information to reporters and activists. "Just

in the past year or two," according to Baumann, "there has been a tremendous increase in awareness of *maquilas*. Within the United States, concerned groups are starting to talk more to each other. We feel that a *maquila* movement is beginning to get off the ground."

Recently, several consultations have brought together researchers and staff of unions, religious organizations, and community groups, to further the process of networking and coordination. "The challenge that faces all of us right now is to define a strategy for coming to terms with the *maquilas*," says Baumann. "It is not realistic to think that we can stop U.S. industry from moving to Mexico. But we can increase solidarity and cross-border communication, and we can place more demands on U.S.-based corporations for accountability."

AFSC is also concerned to connect the emerging *maquila* network with workers, activists, and researchers facing similar issues in other parts of the world. This is a key focus for AFSC's Women and Global Corporations Project, which was also founded in 1978 as part of the group's Nationwide Women's Program (NWP). Through informal networking and a quarterly bulletin, the project works to encourage ongoing international dialog among women in feminist, labor, religious, peace, development, and human rights groups. Notes NWP coordinator Saralee Hamilton, "More and more women are identifying a need to confront the human costs of corporate power, inside and outside the workplace."

The View from El Paso

For those who live and work at the border, the *maquila* economy is an ever-present reality. And unionists in border towns like El Paso are among the most active in cross-border organizing. To call attention to *maquila* issues, the El Paso Central Labor Council—a local grouping of AFL-CIO affiliates—has sponsored demonstrations blocking the bridge to Juárez. In July 1988, El Paso unionists brought thousands of pounds of food to donate to striking workers in Juárez.

More recently, the El Paso union council held a press conference inside Juárez to express their support for an independent union there. The closeness of the two communities—as well as the family, cultural, and language ties between El Paso's many Chicano workers and their Mexican neigh-

---

THE LOSS IS TREMENDOUS

"The loss of jobs is tremendous here. We've had people without a job now for five, six years, due primarily to the maquila industry. They've seen their jobs picked up out of El Paso and taken to Juárez. This dream that we had, that we were supposed to have some jobs here, has just not materialized at all. Yes, here are the few executive positions open here that bring in dollars, but the masses are still going hungry."

—Union activist, El Paso, Texas

bors—has made cross-border communication easy and informal.

This ease of communication makes El Paso one of the few U.S. communities where cross-border interaction also reaches nonunionized workers. "We've learned a lot from groups on the Mexican side," comments Cecilia Rodriguez, "including many of our most valuable lessons." Rodriguez is director of La Mujer Obrera (The Woman Worker), an El Paso center for garment and textile workers, 85 percent of whom are women, mostly Chicanas.

It is not too many years since El Paso, with its thickly clustered garment plants, was known as the "Jeans Capital of the World." Then, in 1985 and 1986, more than 13,000 workers were laid off. Many of the plants moved just across the border to Juárez. Today, says Rodriguez, some jobs are returning—but "the new jobs offer no benefits, no guarantees to the workers. Employment in the industry is still very unstable.

"Given the economic situation in the textile industry," Rodriguez continues, "the unions don't know what to do. They are at a loss. We feel that we have to develop new strategies—and also challenge the unions to respond better to the needs of unorganized workers."

One approach taken by La Mujer Obrera is organizing workers' committees inside the textile plants. "The first goal for these committees," says Rodriguez, "is to pressure the companies to publish personnel policies. The way things work now in the sweatshops is that the owners have total control—they do what they want, when they want. We have a suit pending in the Texas Supreme Court, in which we argue that personnel policies should have contractual force." The suit stems from a 1985 case in which CMT Industries, a local garment manufacturer, promised its workforce a paid holiday for Labor Day and then reneged after they had already taken the day off.

Already, the factory committees have won several rulings from the Texas Employment Commission and the National Labor Relations Board. Union affiliation may be an option for the long term, says Rodriguez, "but in our present situation, it's just not realistic."

Work inside the plants is complemented by a strong emphasis on leadership training and organizational development. "The economic devastation of our communities cannot be described," says Rodriguez. "It is like living after a war. To survive as a

EARL DOTTER

community, we need people with certain skills—organizing, or technical skills like translating or grant-writing. It is very hard to find people who can do these things but who also respect textile workers and believe that they are human beings. If we can train the workers themselves in these skills, three quarters of our battle is won."

A Women-of-Color Network

This emphasis on organizational development has prompted La Mujer Obrera to form a network with other women-of-color organizations in Texas, New Mexico, and California. "For women of color," says Rodriguez, "these questions are not being addressed on a national level, and we cannot tackle them by ourselves on a local level. We need to understand what is going on with multinational corporations and what strategies will allow us to deal with them."

Rodriguez cites the example of another member of the network, a Navajo women weavers' cooperative in New Mexico. "The tribal government has an economic development strategy," she observes, "but the community doesn't really understand what it is. They are talking about developing free

Working and living conditions for U.S. garment workers are often very similar to those of their counterparts in other countries. Yet such workers are among the least likely to have direct access to international interchanges.

trade zones inside Indian reservations—just like on the border. People need to understand what that means."

To sustain itself over the long haul, Rodriguez believes that groups like La Mujer Obrera also need to attend to their own economic base. "The future for groups like ours is not very bright," she comments. "Funding is drying up. Our newest campaign is to start some small economic projects that could provide a permanent income base for us."

In all of these approaches, La Mujer Obrera has been heavily influenced by its connections with Mexican women's groups. Notes Rodriguez: "We've learned from working with them the importance of building in leadership, a political analysis, and a long-term perspective when you're trying to build an organization. We've begun to integrate more economic analysis into our work. We've learned to use a popular education approach" that teaches skills for critical thinking based on people's own life experiences.

"When you're dealing with multinational corporations," Rodriguez concludes, "you can't be complacent. It's a big help to us to be on the border. Our situation is difficult, politically and economically, but we have the advantage of being exposed to a model of organizing that comes from a Third World country."

In some ways, however, La Mujer Obrera is the exception that proves the rule. A majority of U.S. workers touched by the global factory are not reached by unions. This is especially true for women workers. When they organize, it is more likely to be through small, community-based groups than through traditional trade unions.

Such grassroots organizations often develop the most creative strategies for meeting the needs of unorganized workers. They are also far more likely to appreciate the problems women face in combining family and workplace responsibilities. Because they lack an institutional base, however, they tend to be poor in resources, and they seldom have access to international channels of communication.

The same problem exists on the Mexican side of the border. Both Cecilia Rodriguez and UE's Amy Newell say that the Mexican groups they feel closest to are informal bodies that operate outside of any institutional structures. They too are bypassed by formal trade-union channels, and they too lack resources of their own for international networking.

The problem is redoubled for grassroots groups in other Third World countries, which are farther from the United States than Mexico is both in distance and in culture. Thus, for groups that seek to organize around the global factory, a central challenge is how grassroots groups and unorganized workers can be included in any international dialog.

BUILDING INTERNATIONAL NETWORKS

Sister Unions and Solidarity

In part, labor's increasing focus on *maquilas* has been spurred by the sharp increase in the number of U.S. manufacturers moving across the border. Another factor, however, has been the growing concern among labor activists about international issues.

Within the labor movement today, there is more debate than ever before about the meaning and direction of international labor solidarity. A major spur for such debate has been deepening U.S. intervention in Central America, and the wars that have resulted in El Salvador, Nicaragua, and Guatemala. The role of U.S.-based corporations in South Africa has had a similar impact.

Like a large majority of U.S.-Americans, many union members are strongly opposed to the U.S. role in Central America. As a result, union locals across the country, as well as some national unions, have gone on record condemning U.S. financing of the Nicaraguan contras. Another issue has been the systematic violation of human rights, including labor rights, by the U.S.-backed government of El Salvador. In that country, countless trade unionists are among the 80,000 people who have been kidnapped, tortured, and murdered by their own government. Likewise, one recent account tells of a new saying in Guatemala: "If you want to meet a trade union leader, go visit a graveyard."

U.S. labor activism on Central America has been multifaceted. Many unions and labor activists have joined together in a national Labor Committee in Support of Democracy and Human Rights in El Salvador. This group has sponsored delegations of U.S. unionists to visit Central America and has organized speaking tours of Central American union figures in the United States.

Some locals have also formed "sister union" relationships with counterparts in Central America. Such sister unions have lent direct support to each other's strikes. U.S. sister unions have helped publicize the repression of unions or labor activists in Central America. When the employer is linked to a U.S.-based transnational corporation, such publicity can have a significant impact.

In 1986, for example, STITAS, the Salvadoran textile workers union, struck the Circas Corporation, a San Salvador jeans factory. The strike was settled successfully when the California Joint Board of ACTWU, the STITAS sister union, brought pressure to bear on Levi Strauss, which buys jeans from Circas. Women in the STITAS strike were able to win nearly all of their demands. Then, when Circas management took advantage of an earthquake to fire twenty-six union activists—claiming damages to the factory necessitated the layoffs—additional pressure helped win their jobs back for half of the women.

Calling Time on Apartheid

A similar movement is growing to connect U.S. unions with opponents of apartheid in South Africa. Some key national unions—including the United Mineworkers (UMW), UAW, ACTWU, and others—have taken strong stands against the apartheid system of white minority rule and South Africa's harsh repression of Black trade unionists. In many local communities, anti-apartheid labor groups have sponsored rallies, speaking tours, and other educational events.

Like the anti-apartheid movement as a whole, labor groups have focused particular attention on the role of TNCs in propping up apartheid. In campuses and communities across the country, labor has joined local coalitions demanding divestment from companies that do business with South Africa. On a national level, unions have fought for comprehensive sanctions legislation banning all forms of corporate involvement with the apartheid economy. The UMW has coordi-

EARL DOTTER

nated a national boycott of Shell Oil, a major TNC that has refused to withdraw from South Africa. This campaign has been particularly successful in forging a coalition between labor and other constituencies.

In June 1989, the anti-apartheid movement scored a major victory when Mobil Oil sold off all its assets in South Africa. Not only did Mobil divest, it also became the first TNC to agree to negotiate the terms of its withdrawal with the South African workers who would be affected, members of the Chemical Workers Industrial Union. Such negotiations had been a principal demand of the labor and religious groups that were pressuring Mobil to divest.

Some labor groups, reports Kate Pfordresher of New York's Labor Committee Against Apartheid (LCAA), are also pressing for the inclusion of labor rights provisions in anti-apartheid legislation. This approach, says Pfordresher, "will allow us to bring the issue even closer to the management performance" of specific TNCs. The strategy is patterned on successful attempts to include support for labor rights in U.S. trade policy (see box on page 72).

Once anti-apartheid laws or codes are passed, union activists can play a special role in pressing for their enforcement. In a recent case reported by the LCAA, union technicians at the city's Bellevue Hospital learned of the planned purchase of eight new electrocardiogram machines from Hewlett-Packard, a U.S.-based TNC that operates in South Africa.

Officials of the Health and Hospitals Corporation (HHC), a city agency, refused to concede that New York's anti-apartheid purchasing law covered this case, and al-

Union demonstrators protest U.S. intervention in El Salvador.

lowed the sale to go through. However, as a result of pressure from the Bellevue workers, who were members of Teamsters Local 237, HHC issued a new policy stating that in the future vendors must be checked for their connections to South Africa before a purchase is approved.

Within the U.S. labor movement, opponents of apartheid, like those seeking to halt U.S. intervention in Central America, are working in concert with many other groups in society. On both of these issues, churches and synagogues, student groups, and community organizations are also broadly involved. Coalition efforts have developed on a variety of specific campaigns.

At times—with the Shell boycott, for example, or a ten-year campaign focused on the activities of Coca Cola in Guatemala—these coalition efforts are directly targeting the role of TNCs. As such, they provide an important foundation for building a movement around the global factory.

The Winds of Change

The emergence of these new solidarity networks has also had a profound impact

Solidarity Success Stories

International pressure campaigns have played a key role in supporting the demands and even saving the lives of Third World labor activists. The stories that follow—one from South Africa, the other from Guatemala—are only two of countless possible examples of effective solidarity efforts.

In South Africa, an extensive international campaign led to the release in early 1989 of labor leader Moses Mayekiso, the general secretary of the National Union of Metalworkers of South Africa (NUMSA). Mayekiso had been imprisoned in June 1986, shortly after the South African government declared a state of emergency in an attempt to break the anti-apartheid movement.

After being held without charges for nearly a year, Mayekiso was accused of treason, for which the penalty is death. His supposedly treasonous activities, detailed in a 163-page indict-ment, included mobilizing support in Britain for a NUMSA strike against a plant in Sarmcol, South Africa, owned by British transnational BTR. The charges were also based on his role as chair of the Alexandra Action Committee, a community-based organization that had led consumer and rent boycotts in Alexandra township.

A worldwide protest of the charges against Mayekiso was organized by the International Metalworkers Federation (IMF). In the United States, the United Auto Workers Union, an affiliate of the IMF, coordinated a national post-card campaign. The UAW also sent a delegation of legal experts to observe the Mayekiso trial. Union activists staged rallies in San Francisco, Detroit, Chicago, and New York.

When Mayekiso finally came to trial in April 1989, he was acquitted of all the charges against him and released from prison. "It was the international support, especially from the labor movement, that led to his acquittal," states Themba Ntinga, a spokesman for the African National Council. "Without this kind of visibility, he would have been convicted."

Ntinga adds, "There have been other trials of labor leaders. The offices of COSATU (the Congress of South African Trade Unions) were blown up last year by agents of the apartheid regime. As this occurs, international support for the anti-apartheid movement, particularly from labor, is large and growing. This is what makes it possible for COSATU to sustain its battles."

In Guatemala, strikers at a textile plant known as Lunafil were able to protect their jobs and win virtually all of their demands, thanks in part to a solidarity campaign coordinated by the U.S./Guatemala Labor Education Project (US/GLEP), a national network of U.S. trade unionists.

The Lunafil strike was touched off when management tried to impose a new schedule that would have forced employees to work twelve-hour shifts on both Saturday and Sunday, with no overtime pay. Ninety-one workers sat

(continued on next page)

on the U.S. labor movement as a whole. To an unprecedented degree, rank-and-file unionists and unions at the local level have become actively involved in direct international communication. One result has been a challenge to some of the long-standing orthodoxies of AFL-CIO foreign policy.

Throughout the era of the Cold War, the world's labor movements have been divided along political lines into competing international groupings. National labor confederations from the United States and its allies are grouped together in the International Confederation of Free Trade Unions (ICFTU).

This body was formed in 1949 as a breakaway from the World Federation of Trade Unions (WFTU), amid postwar conflicts between the AFL and left-leaning labor movements in many western European countries. Today, the WFTU groups together labor confederations from the Soviet Union and its allies.

Traditionally, international contacts for U.S. unions have been channeled through the AFL-CIO, which has worked to discourage communication with foreign unions outside the ICFTU. Now, many trade unionists are beginning to question these restrictions.

(continued from last page)

down and occupied the factory—a daring tactic in Guatemala, where labor activists have been a key target of the death squads that have murdered tens of thousands of civilians in the past decade.

A month into the strike, management announced the plant was permanently closed and attempted to evict the strikers with the aid of armed security guards. Nonetheless, the strikers continued to occupy part of the plant, the courtyard, and the gate, which gave them access to the outside world. In the end, thirty-nine workers maintained the sit-in for over a year.

From the beginning, U.S. unionists had sent telegrams of support for the strikers to Lunafil management and Guatemala's president and labor minister. Union officials signed newspaper advertisements denouncing the use of armed paramilitary guards and other attacks against the Lunafil strikers. As the strike wore on, support was organized from unionists in several western European countries as well. Inside Guatemala, other unions and community groups also mobilized for an active solidarity campaign.

While this international visibility undoubtedly prevented violent repression of the strike, it was not sufficient to force a settlement. Eventually, US/

GLEP turned to a corporate campaign, focusing pressure on the U.S. connections of Lunafil's shareholders. One major shareholder, Julio Raul Herrera, was a Washington lobbyist for Guatemalan sugar interests. As a result of US/GLEP efforts, six U.S. congresspeople sent Herrera a telegram demanding a prompt settlement of the strike and questioning his "ability to act as an effective spokesperson for the Guatemalan sugar industry."

At that point, serious negotiations finally began. In July 1988, an agreement was signed that reinstated the strikers and limited the workweek to forty-four hours, Guatemala's legal maximum. Further pressure was required to force the agreement's implementation three months later.

In an account of the Lunafil strike published in the *Labor Research Review'* US/GLEP executive director Peter Hogness argues that such actions directly benefit U.S. workers as well as their Third World counterparts. "The worse conditions are abroad for clothing and textile workers," writes Hogness, "the more likely U.S. companies are to move production overseas. The more we help foreign workers . . . to defend their rights and raise their living standards, the more likely it is that we can preserve those jobs in the U.S."

IUE members demonstrate in Washington, DC to protest the role of Shell Oil in the South African economy.

At a recent convention, for example, the Service Employees International Union (SEIU) voted to work not just with ICFTU affiliates but with "any other group that supports the principles of peace, democracy, and economic justice." This resolution grew directly out of a conflict over the relationship between some SEIU locals and UNTS, a nonaligned Salvadoran labor confederation opposed by AFL-CIO leadership.

For the past few years, the annual conventions of the AFL-CIO itself have been marked by heated debates over contra aid and other Central America issues. Formal resolutions have been moving in the direction of opposing U.S. intervention in Central America.

The AFL-CIO has also come out in support of comprehensive sanctions against South Africa, reversing its previous position. According to the LCAA's Kate Pfordresher, the reversal shows that the AFL-CIO "recognizes that for many Black union members, opposing apartheid is an issue of overriding importance. It also indicates that anti-apartheid activities at the local level are having an impact nationally."

In addition, recent AFL-CIO statements have been far more supportive of COSATU, South Africa's largest labor federation. Within South Africa, COSATU is one of apartheid's most powerful opponents. However, like El Salvador's UNTS, COSATU is not aligned with either the ICFTU or the WFTU—which so far has disqualified both federations for formal relations with the AFL-CIO.

The Debate Expands

The growing debate over labor's foreign policy has everything to do with TNCs. In both South Africa and Central America, TNC workers are among the most determined advocates of basic social change. And many of the particular struggles, small and large, that make up the social movements in each region target specific TNCs through their subsidiaries or contractors.

Meanwhile, U.S. unionists have found that when it comes to organizing against the TNCs, the foreign unions endorsed by the AFL-CIO may not be the most effective allies for U.S. workers. Throughout the Third World, ICFTU affiliates most often group together unions that have backing from their own local governments. These governments, as described in chapter 1, are frequently beholden to TNCs as a source of badly needed jobs and foreign exchange.

Traditionally, the AFL-CIO has worked internationally to support national security interests as defined by the U.S. government. Throughout the post-World War II era, the labor federation has been a pillar of the Cold War consensus that has placed anti-communism above all other foreign policy considerations. At times, its international activities have been linked to the CIA, especially through such bodies as the American Institute for Free Labor Development (AIFLD) in Latin America or the Asian-American Free Labor Institute (AAFLI). These agencies are sponsored by the AFL-CIO but primarily funded by the U.S. government.

Today, many U.S. unionists are more concerned with TNCs than with the Cold War vision of rivalry between the United States and the Soviet Union. As a result, they are calling for increased flexibility in international labor contacts.

One organization that has helped bring about more open communication is the Transnational Information Exchange (TIE), which is based in Amsterdam. Through TIE, rank-and-file workers from many countries can meet to discuss developments in their industries, comparing notes on new technology, management strategies, and the like. Recently, TIE has sponsored small working conferences for telecommunications workers and also for auto workers. Both conferences have brought together unionists from the Third World with their counterparts from advanced industrial countries, regardless of traditional political divisions.

Corporate Responsibility:
The Religious Community Responds

Since 1976, the Interfaith Center for Corporate Responsibility (ICCR) has used the financial muscle of mainstream U.S. churches to pressure many major TNCs to address questions of workers' rights and other social justice issues. "Individuals very seldom have the ability," notes ICCR staffperson Dara Deming, "to make their concerns heard by corporate management. This is where churches have a special role to play," because of their status as institutional investors.

As shareholders in many large corporations, ICCR members can introduce resolutions at annual corporate meetings—calling for divestment from South Africa, requiring management to make more purchases from minority contractors, or advocating the concerns of workers at an overseas plant. Depending on the issue, ICCR may also sponsor hearings, support consumer boycotts, help organize demonstrations, or even work with management informally to develop more enlightened policies.

Currently, ICCR's main concerns include promoting the withdrawal of TNCs from South Africa, easing the international debt crisis, promoting affirmative action, and seeking improved working conditions for Third World women employed by U.S.-based corporations. The role of TNCs in nuclear weapons and space weaponry is another area of concern.

In Korea, for example, when the Tandy Corporation, operators of Radio Shack, shut down a plant in mid-1989 without paying severance, ICCR began a campaign to pressure the company either to reopen the plant or to make the severance payments. "We are also calling on management," says Demings, "to recognize the principles of fair treatment to workers—including adequate wages, health and safety standards, and the right to organize."

ICCR, which groups together well over 200 religious congregations and agencies, is a strong believer in coalitions and frequently works in coordination with labor, community, and other religious groups.

One such campaign is directed at Manufacturers Hanover Trust, a bank with over $210 million invested in the South African economy. According to ICCR's Donna Katzin, this campaign illustrates the many possibilities for linking issues and working in coalition that may be presented by TNCs.

"Manufacturers Hanover," notes Katzin, "has helped South Africa by rescheduling one-year loans into ten-year loans. We're calling on them to demand rapid repayment of these loans." ICCR is coordinating its efforts with religious groups in West Germany, Switzerland, France, and Britain—all countries where major banks are holding extensive South African debt.

Domestically, Manufacturers Hanover has extended a $100 million line of credit to the Pittston Co.—currently the object of a protracted and bitter strike by thousands of members of the United Mine Workers (UMW) union throughout Appalachia. The strike was provoked when the company unilaterally cut wages and cancelled pension and health benefits—a move that was widely seen as an attempt to break the back of the UMW. "The $100 million credit was granted one month before the strike," observes Katzin, "and Pittston is still drawing on that credit. It's definitely helping the company hold out."

Another face of the campaign has emerged in the New York City borough of Brooklyn, where UMW has joined forces with community groups to oppose the bank's illegal redlining. Currently, Manufacturers Hanover is seeking to acquire eleven Brooklyn branches of Gold Dome Federal Savings. Yet, notes Katzin, "while Manufacturers Hanover holds billions of dollars in deposits from poor and working class people in Brooklyn, its total reinvestment there is less than $3 million." The federal Community Reinvestment Act prohibits banks from making acquisitions in areas they redline, providing a domestic angle for the Manufacturers Hanover campaign.

In a remote Philippine village, a member of the peasant organization KMP tells U.S. visitors about the negative impact of U.S. military bases on the country's women and children.

To keep up with the transnationals, unions have also become more sophisticated in using modern information technology. Within the ICFTU, industry subgroups are using computer networks to allow unions from different countries to compare notes on the operations of particular TNCs.

Yet, say some activists, much more remains to be done to develop adequate strategies. Comments Jeff Stansbury of the International Ladies Garment Workers Union: "In general, the TNCs have been ten to twenty years ahead of their opponents. You can be sure that industry is already planning where and how it will be moving ten years from now, but we're hardly even thinking about it yet." In many countries, for example, organizing in the global electronics industry began as a result of massive worldwide layoffs in the early and middle 1980s. The companies were already leaving by the time the workers' movements began.

"The only way we can develop that kind of strategic thinking," Stansbury believes, "is to communicate much more closely with workers everywhere. In the long run," he predicts, "we'll have to move beyond cooperation and networking to internationally coordinated organizing."

The Next Arena for Intervention

The Philippines may well become another significant focus of controversy within the labor movement. In that country, the AFL-CIO is aligned with the official labor confederation, the Trade Union Congress of the Philippines (TUCP). However, in the opinion of John Witeck, a spokesman for the Philippine Workers Solidarity Commit-

tee (PWSC) in Honolulu, U.S. workers would be better served by developing ties with a rival confederation, the KMU (Kilusang Mayo Uno, or May First Movement).

"The TUCP," says Witeck, "has been linked to the Philippine military and the vigilante groups," which operate similarly to death squads in Central America. "What's more, it supports multinational corporations in policies that are detrimental to workers in both the Philippines and the United States.

"The same corporations," Witeck emphasizes, "are harming workers in both countries. It's in our own interest to support Filipino workers—it's not just charity."

Since 1983, PWSC has been working to bring KMU speakers to U.S. unions, as well as encouraging U.S. unionists to visit the Philippines. Where unions are already working on South Africa or Central America issues, says Witeck, "they are the most open to meeting Philippine unionists." Progress is difficult, he notes, because "the AFL-CIO has taken a particularly hard line against the KMU, branding it as a 'communist front' organization."

Founded in Honolulu, PWSC has grown to include chapters in New York, Boston, Seattle, and Oakland, California. While focused on work within the labor movement, the group also has participated in a variety of coalition efforts. Through the Food and Freedom Fund for the island of Negros, says Witeck, PWSC has worked with several church groups to raise $150,000 over two years. The fund supports the cooperative farmlot program of the Philippines' National Federation of Sugar Workers, a KMU affiliate.

In Hawaii, PWSC has also supported the Filipino Women and Children's Project, an effort involving the state's large Filipino immigrant community. This project channels funds to a Manila-based support center for prostitutes, their children, and street youth. In this case, notes Witeck, "most of the fundraising has been carried out through cultural programs by the local Filipino community."

Although the Philippines receives little attention in the United States, Witeck feels that groups like PWSC are badly needed. "The Philippines is a very rich country with very poor people," he observes. "There is a long relationship between the Philippines and the United States. The U.S. government has tremendous dominance over Philippine policy, and a large number of U.S. transnationals are doing business there. Right now a lot of workers and farmers are being repressed. Unless considerable education and support work is carried out in the United States, the Philippines is likely to become a major arena for U.S. military intervention."

Travel to the Philippines is expensive, and Witeck estimates that no more than thirty U.S. unionists have visited there with PWSC sponsorship. But those who have made the trip, he says, "have come back feeling rejuvenated in unionism. People have learned a lot from seeing the KMU's emphasis on the total picture. The KMU has a point of view about land reform, about what kind of industrialization is needed in the Philippines. They also place a lot of importance on rank-and-file education and democracy."

Connecting women unionists in the United States and the Philippines has been a priority for PWSC. "When you go to the Philippines," comments Witeck, "you see that in the factories and on the picket lines, at least 70 percent of the activists are women, mostly under twenty-five. This is not yet reflected in the KMU National Council, which is 80 percent men. But at the level of action, the leadership is women."

Overall, Witeck feels, women in the KMU "are slowly growing as a force." On a national level, the KMU has raised a demand

REBECCA RATCLIFF

for four months of paid maternity leave. "This has become an issue in nearly all contract bargaining," notes Witeck. Already, PWSC has sponsored a prominent Filipina activist to speak to the national convention of the Coalition of Labor Union Women. For 1990, PWSC is planning a speaking tour for representatives of the KMK, a women's organization affiliated with the KMU.

KMK members in Mindanao prepare for a rally.

NEW CHALLENGES, NEW STRATEGIES

Women and Microtechnology

As described in chapter 4, many women workers in the Philippines are employed by TNCs, working in sweatshop conditions in special areas known as export processing zones (EPZs). It was inside these zones that the KMK, or Women Workers Movement, was founded in 1984. The experience of working in the EPZs has been a strong incentive for Philippine women to reach out for bonds of international solidarity.

For women in the EPZs, the global factory is a daily reality. The companies they work for are headquartered in the United States, Japan, or other advanced industrial countries. Their jobs involve assembling goods for foreign markets, using foreign components. When women organize to demand better conditions, they often receive threats that their jobs will move to yet another country.

Like women workers the world over, KMK activists have found that women's needs are best served by a dual strategy, working both inside and outside of union structures. Internationally, many of the women the KMK has the most in common with are not union members. Such women generally cannot be reached through existing labor networks.

In some cases, international feminist networks have provided an alternative channel of communication. An example of this approach was a 1986 conference in the Philippines on "Microchip Technology: Its Impact on Women Workers." This ten-day meeting was jointly sponsored by the KMK, the Women's Program of the International Council for Adult Education, and women's resource centers in the Philippines and Canada.

The conference brought together organizers, labor educators, and rank-and-file workers, with experiences ranging from microchip production in Asia to clerical jobs in Canada and the United States that have been transformed by microchip-based technology. Participants came from half a dozen Asian countries, the Caribbean basin, and the Netherlands, as well as from North America.

The microtechnology conference was designed to launch an international network that would bring together women workers in both the electronics industry and the automated office. The results of the meeting illustrate both the difficulties and the importance of reaching out to unorganized workers, in the United States and internationally.

Solidarity Begins at Home

Overall, the idea of forming an ongoing international network was premature, concedes Carol-Anne Douglas of the Participatory Research Group in Toronto, which helped to organize the meeting. "In North America," says Douglas, "we found that we lacked an organizational framework that could coordinate follow-up. We realized that we were not sufficiently integrated with the labor movement.

"Some of the Asian women," Douglas adds, "continued to stay in touch for a year or so after the meeting. But the repression they face has increased so much that many

The Labor Rights Strategy

"For years," comments John Cavanaugh, "many of us were looking for a way to put some teeth in human rights legislation. We won some nice language in the 1970s, but it didn't have much real impact on U.S. foreign policy. Our success began when we started talking about workers rights as an important part of human rights."

Cavanaugh is on the staff of the Institute for Policy Studies (IPS), a progressive think-tank in Washington, DC. In 1984, IPS came together with a broad range of labor, religious, and human rights organizations to form the International Labor Rights Working Group (ILRWG). Already, the coalition has successfully lobbied the U.S. Congress to include labor rights clauses in four major pieces of U.S. trade policy.

The first victory came in 1984, when a labor rights provision was included in the Generalized System of Preferences (GSP). Under the GSP, certain Third World countries can export products to the United States without paying import duties. Notes Cavanaugh: "The top beneficiaries of the GSP have been corporations based in Taiwan and South Korea, both horrendous violators of labor rights. This means that those corporations can gain an unfair advantage by exploiting workers."

Now, with the labor rights provision, if the State Department finds that a country does not respect workers' rights, it is automatically excluded

from participation in the GSP. One of the strengths of the law is that the initiative for enforcement does not rest only with the U.S. government. Any group can file a petition accusing a country of violations. Then, explains Cavanaugh, "the government has to investigate and make a determination."

Some Third World governments have charged that the labor rights legislation is interventionist, imposing U.S. standards on other parts of the world. But, notes Cavanaugh, "we're not using U.S. definitions. The definition of labor rights follows the standards of the International Labor Organization," an agency of the United Nations. The rights that are specified include prohibitions on forced labor and child labor, as well as protection of the right to organize unions and bargain collectively.

"As long as transnational corporations can go anywhere in the world," says Cavanaugh, "one of two things has to happen. Either living standards will go down in developed countries—that's what is happening now. Or they will rise in Third World countries. That's what this legislation is designed to encourage."

After a long pressure campaign, Chile, one of the world's harshest dictatorships, was eliminated from the GSP. Next, a major conflict was sparked when Americas Watch, a human rights group, filed a petition charging the government of El Salvador with sys-

(continued on next page)

roups are no longer able to be active.'' Waves of arrests have stymied labor activists in Malaysia, Singapore, and Indonesia. In the Philippines, key labor and women's organizations have been declared undesirable by the government and violently attacked by local vigilante groups.

Douglas's judgment is borne out by the experience of U.S. women who attended the microtechnology meeting. One U.S. participant was Lisa Gallatin, who staffs the Office Technology Education Project (OTEP) in the Boston area. Although Gallatin believes her trip was valuable, the relative absence of unions among her constituency makes follow-up difficult.

Office workers, explains Gallatin, are organized mainly in the public sector; with a few exceptions, unions have not gained a foothold among private-sector office workers. OTEP's overall strategy is to reach out to unorganized workers through educational programs. "We help women understand the health effects of new office technology," she notes, "and also its impact on how jobs are structured. We can also provide organizing assistance for office workers who are trying to improve their situation."

For Gallatin, the experience of attending the microchip conference was "thrilling, and even more eye-opening than I expected. What sticks in my mind the most," she

---

(continued from previous page)
tematic violations of labor rights. After an initial review, the U.S. Trade Representative, the office charged with enforcing the law, declined to hold public hearings. Comments ILRWG's Kathy Selvaggio: "We learned from the experience with El Salvador that we need a lot of grassroots pressure to make the law work. Advocacy groups in Washington can't make it happen alone."

Since the first victory with the GSP, similar provisions have been added to two other important pieces of legislation. The 1988 trade act defines violations of labor rights as an unfair trade practice. And a labor rights requirement has also been imposed on the Overseas Private Investment Corporation, a government agency that insures U.S.-based transnational corporations operating in the Third World.

The ILRWG's next target is the General Agreement on Trade and Tariffs (GATT), a multilateral trade pact that includes the United States and many governments it considers friendly. "In GATT," notes Cavanaugh, "this approach was suggested fifteen years ago by Sweden and blocked by the United States. Now the U.S. Congress has mandated U.S. support for a labor rights clause." For the future, adds Cavanaugh, "we're also looking at articles 806 and 807 of the tariff code," the U.S. regulations that govern the *maquiladora* program on the Mexico-U.S. border.

The breadth of the ILRWG coalition, Cavanaugh believes, is one reason the group has enjoyed a string of successes. The group brings together many major trade unions from inside and outside the AFL-CIO, as well as large religious denominations such as the United Methodist Church. The human rights community is represented by groups like Americas Watch as well as organizations devoted to particular countries, including the Washington Office on Haiti, the Church Coalition for Human Rights in the Philippines, and others. Some former human rights officials from the Carter Administration are also included, as are a few representatives of business. The group's efforts have been actively supported by Rep. Don Pease (D-Ohio), a key congressional figure on trade issues.

One drawback of the ILRWG approach may be the very openness of the procedure for enforcing labor rights through the GSP. Already, a petition filed by the Heritage Foundation has caused Rumania to be dropped from the GSP program. Nicaragua has also been excluded, as a result of a petition from the AFL-CIO.

For Nicaragua, the move "is mainly symbolic," says Cavanaugh, "because trade with Nicaragua is already completely embargoed." Nonetheless, some ILRWG members are fighting to have the restriction lifted. "It is obviously biased," Cavanaugh believes, "to say that Nicaragua does not respect basic workers rights."

Workers at the Oohri Data Company in Kwang-Ju, South Korea, occupied their workplace when their employer announced the office was closing. Women here earned $1 to $1.50 an hour entering the text of English-language medical and reference books onto computer disks for U.S. publishers.

comments, "is how much women workers have in common, despite the many differences between the First and Third World. In both contexts, women are concerned with health issues, childcare, sexual harassment, pay and benefits, and job security."

In addition, notes Gallatin, "management strategies for discouraging unions are also very similar. Sometimes it's 'we're all one big happy family,' and sometimes it's 'we'll move out of the country and you'll lose your job.' I didn't realize before how multinationals hop from country to country all over the world—it's not just workers in the United States who are left behind."

When Gallatin returned home, she spoke widely about her experience, showing slides to rank-and-file office workers, union groups, and women's organizations. "Talking about the Philippines and the movement there," she recalls, "gave us a way to talk much more deeply about the global economy. We looked at how the automated office is also tied into these worldwide trends. Information processing is like assembly work—it can be done anywhere in the world now, because of computer and satellite technology. Both ends of the global assembly line—the production work and the information processing—employ mainly women in very low-paying jobs."

Under present conditions, believes Gallatin, international networking is still a distant goal. In the United States, she says, the weakness of unions themselves is the limiting factor. "The service sector as a whole has been neglected by the labor movement. As a result, unions often have a negative image and many office workers do not realize what unions could offer them."

As Gallatin spoke with OTEP supporters about the lessons of her trip, "we talked a

lot about the need we saw for building international solidarity. But we realized that is a long process—and the first step is building solidarity among unions and other organizations here in Massachusetts." In this line, a key priority for OTEP is strengthening the Massachusetts Coalition on New Office Technology, a two-year-old body that brings together union locals, women's organizations, and other groups.

"The purpose of this coalition," says Gallatin, "is to bring together organized and unorganized office workers. We want to be accessible to the vast majority of office workers, who are not unionized." Currently the coalition is pressing for legislation to restrict the electronic monitoring of clerical workers. Without more progress on the home front, Gallatin believes, there is little opportunity to proceed with international contacts.

A Step Ahead of the Sheriff

Many of Gallatin's observations are echoed by Amanda Hawes, a Silicon Valley lawyer who also attended the microtechnology conference. Hawes has represented many electronics workers who have been injured by exposure to toxic compounds. She is also the board president of the Santa Clara Center for Occupational Safety and Health (SCCOSH), which focuses on health hazards in California's electronics industry.

At the conference, recalls Hawes, "I was able to share a lot of what we've learned about chemical hazards. The women from Asia found this helpful, because for them it is difficult to obtain such information. For me, it was very useful to look at the broader perspective of how the industry operates worldwide. I was also very moved by the spirit of the people I met. But it's difficult to say how we could follow up. Our work in California simply does not reach that level."

Hawes describes SCCOSH's efforts as "trench warfare against the industry on behalf of individual people whose lives are being wrecked. Not only women but also their unborn children are threatened." In addition to fighting for workers' compensation or disability benefits for individuals, SCCOSH has also conducted wider campaigns for restrictions on specific chemicals. "But when we succeed in eliminating one hazard, they switch to something else," she says. "They're keeping one step ahead of the sheriff."

Hawes sees a lot of changes in awareness of the threat to workers. "The electronics industry," she comments, "has lost its image as a clean industry, with both workers and many health professionals. But over the long term, workers cannot protect themselves effectively without collective bargaining. And in fifteen years, no one has succeeded in organizing a union among production workers in Silicon Valley."

Likewise, the absence of unions leaves workers without any mechanism to pursue international contacts. "Until we learn how to organize here," Hawes asserts, "international solidarity will remain more of a vision than a reality."

Reaching Every Worker

Like many activists in the same bind, Hawes has come to believe in the necessity of exploring alternative organizing strategies. In Silicon Valley, she notes, many production workers are recent immigrants. Thus, classes that teach English as a Second Language (ESL) may be a way of reaching workers who cannot be reached by traditional union approaches.

Many ESL teachers, Hawes has found, would like to use teaching materials that have more relevance to the lives of their students. "If we can teach about occupational health through ESL classes," she says, "then the students can take this information back to their own communities." Creating this new channel of communication could eventually lay the basis for coalition efforts among unions, groups like SCCOSH, church-based and community groups, and immigrant communities.

In the spring of 1988, the Highlander Center, an adult education center in Tennessee, suggested this approach to activists from across the United States at a workshop entitled "Reaching Every Worker." Hawes, who attended the workshop, has already taught one such class and plans to continue.

The lessons of OTEP, SCCOSH, and the microtechnology conference parallel the experience of groups reaching out to *maquila* workers in Mexico. To make significant headway, efforts to organize in the global factory must find new ways of reaching out to workers who are women, recent immigrants, and people of color. These groups make up a large portion of the transnational workforce in the United States—and are the least likely to be unionized of all U.S. workers.

Domestically, cooperative efforts between labor and many different kinds of community groups have proven to be the surest way to reach out to the unorganized. These innovative efforts can also provide a channel for international outreach and communication.

In general, the conditions do not exist for drawing nonunionized U.S. workers into ongoing international networks. But some labor and religious groups do have the capacity to include nonunion workers in speaking tours, educational programs, and visits to other countries. In this way, groups with greater institutional resources can help lay the groundwork for a more broadly based international solidarity.

THE CHALLENGE CONTINUES

Each of the projects we have described may seem tiny, especially when contrasted to the size and power of transnational corporations. Yet each is also a small step toward building a movement that could bring together hundreds of local grassroots campaigns, within the United States and internationally.

At this writing, the idea of a broad-based, multinational movement to tackle the problems of the global factory is still a vision. What we have tried to document in this guide is that the global factory is composed of thousands of concrete local situations—and that each of us, whatever setting we live and work in, can take small, accessible actions to confront our specific situations.

By understanding that every local story is part of a global "big picture," we can open up space for dialog and sharing of experiences—especially across the barriers of language, nationality, gender, race, and class. And as that process of communication moves toward networking and coalition-building, the vision of a multinational movement can become a reality.

6. Starting a Discussion-Action Project

Previous chapters of this guide have explored the nature of the global factory and the types of activism that have emerged in response to it. This chapter offers suggestions on how to structure educational programs on the global factory—and on how some groups might move from education into action.

People may come together in all kinds of settings to talk about global factory issues. A church group might be studying living and working conditions for people in Third World countries. Union members might be trying to find out what would happen to their jobs if their employer moved to Mexico. A college class might be exploring contemporary developments in the global economy.

Because so many diverse groups have an interest in these questions, we have not attempted to discuss how a group should organize itself or what its focus might be. There are simply too many different answers. Instead, we have tried to make this guide as useful as possible to different types of groups with varying goals and different levels of energy and commitment.

Below, we offer some overall suggestions about how to plan and lead a discussion. The next section suggests sample questions for discussion, and a third section presents a few ideas for longer-term projects.

PLANNING A DISCUSSION: GENERAL SUGGESTIONS

Think about the setting and the goals of your project.

The setting you are working in will shape the scope of your discussion and also its goals. Some groups may be holding a single class or study session, with the aim of educating participants about the existence of the global factory. Their goal might be to encourage people to think about the ethical implications of corporate expansion, for example, or to challenge the notion that foreign workers are "taking away" the jobs of workers in the United States.

Other groups may be planning a longer, more in-depth study program—perhaps with an open-ended goal of seeing whether the group might move into some form of action. Their purpose might be to encourage understanding and potential ties among women from the United States and other countries,

for instance. Or they might be examining the problems faced by U.S. workers who are threatened with the loss of their jobs.

Still other groups are already involved in an ongoing campaign—around a plant closing, say, or in opposition to U.S. involvement in the Philippines—and may be seeking to deepen their own members' understanding of the issues they are grappling with. Such a group might plan one or two educational sessions or a longer project, perhaps with a research component.

If you are planning a discussion, no matter how informal, it is useful to think about who the participants will be, what your goals are as a group, and how much time you will have. Because the global factory affects so many different types of people, the goals of different groups will be extremely diverse. This makes it all the more important to develop a clear idea of what your particular group is working toward. In some cases, it may be helpful to plan some preliminary goals for one or two sessions and then re-examine them, depending on the level of interest that has been sparked.

Think about what other resources you will use.

Whether your project is brief or extended, it will benefit greatly from using films or other audiovisual resources to start off a discussion. By offering images of real people in real circumstances, audiovisuals can add some human flesh and blood onto the bare bones of a global analysis. Such images enable people to respond on an emotional as well as an intellectual level, greatly increasing their interest and sense of involvement in the issues.

There is no one "perfect" audiovisual addressing global economic issues, just as there is no one "perfect" angle from which to approach a discussion. However, one of the films listed in chapter 7—*The Global Assembly Line*—does address many of the issues raised in this guide, providing compelling and evocative images of working women in the U.S. and the Third World and counterposing their experiences against the pronouncements of corporate spokesmen.

Depending on the focus of your group, you may also want to use written testimony to add a "human face" to your program. Excerpts from a booklet like *Tales of the Filipino Working Women*, for example, could provide much of the same sense of immediacy as an audiovisual. Or perhaps there is someone in your community who has slides or videotapes based on personal travels or on organizing experiences around a local issue. Either of these could provide a point of departure for a broader discussion.

Groups that will be meeting over a period of time might want to use a variety of resources to focus attention on different aspects of the issues. Chapter 7 of this guide offers a range of print and audiovisual materials that may be helpful in planning your program.

Focus on the human dimensions of the problem.

No matter what setting you are working in, it is useful to provide an opportunity for people to think out loud about what these global issues mean in their own lives. How

are they or other people in their lives affected by structural unemployment or the replacement of industrial jobs with low-paid service work? What about the transformation of office work by new information technology, or the difficulties faced by many families in surviving on a single income? How has your local community been touched by these trends?

By the same token, the human dimension is crucial in understanding the experiences of working people in other countries. If you have used a video or film that depicts conditions in the Third World, who were some of the individuals you saw? What problems did they face, and how were they attempting to resolve them? What do you imagine their reasons to be for the choices they made?

A particular "human dimension" is that most circumstances affect men and women quite differently. In many situations, the disappearing high-paid jobs are traditionally men's jobs. The new low-paid jobs being created often have a predominantly female workforce. Everywhere women are paid less than men and carry a heavier weight of family responsibilities. How do these gender dynamics affect people in your group? Other people in their lives? People in any films or videos you may have seen together? (Remember that men as well as women are profoundly affected by gender roles in the workplace, family, and community.)

Draw out the beliefs that people bring with them to the discussion.

Many people will come into a discussion with already formed beliefs about global economic issues—beliefs that they may never have examined critically. It is crucial to bring out such beliefs so that the group can take a look at them together. The mass media are especially persistent in promoting ideas that leave people feeling powerless and suspicious of one another. Examples of such ideas include:

• Foreign workers are "taking away" the jobs of workers in the U.S.

• People in the Third World are passive victims of their fate who suffer and starve in silence.

• Women who work paid jobs are "taking away" employment from men who "really need it."

• "Illegal aliens" come to the United States only to get on the welfare rolls.

• Industry is moving out of the United States because U.S. workers have "priced themselves out of the market."

• Labor unions are responsible for the decline of U.S. industry, because of their "unreasonable" wage demands and insistence on "outmoded" work rules.

• U.S. plants are forced to move overseas because of "foreign competition."

• The global factory is an inevitable outcome of "laws of the market" and technological change.

• "The Japanese" are taking over the U.S. economy.

Obviously, not every person or group will hold these views, and many participants may have come to challenge them through previous experiences. Nonetheless, we all live in a media environment where we are constantly bombarded with these ideas, which are never presented as ideology—only as fact.

Many of these ideas serve as a sort of "cover" for racist, sexist, and anti-foreign sentiments. When such prejudices go unexamined, they become a crippling obstacle to effective political action and coalition-building. Worse, they can fuel the growing emotional appeal of violent extremist movements, like "white power" groups in the United States or anti-immigrant organizations in western Europe. Thus, it is important to bring these beliefs into the light so that they may be addressed directly.

You may want to ask people whether they agree or disagree with the statements listed above and what their reasons are. Another approach, if you are using a film or video, might be to ask your group who they identified with in the presentation and why. Or you might want to simply stay attentive to people's comments and questions, choosing an apt moment to draw out some of the assumptions that may underlie them.

A good way to examine these beliefs would be to explore who is responsible for the development of the global factory and the movement of industry out of the United States. There are three questions that are very useful for analyzing the power dynamics of any situation: Who decides? Who benefits? Who pays the price?

Draw out the feelings the global factory brings up for people.

People's emotional reactions offer a rich vein of insight into the opportunities and obstacles we face in seeking to transform our lives and our world. Any time your program brings your group in touch with the human dimension of the global factory, it is highly worthwhile to encourage participants to voice their feelings. Opportune moments may occur after seeing a video or film, during a discussion of how people are personally affected by the global economy, or at other times.

If you are leading a discussion, a first step in being aware of other people's feelings is to examine what feelings the issue brings up for you. For many people, a new understanding of the global economy may conflict with previously held ideas, resulting in confusion and even disbelief. Many feel anger toward transnational corporations and the system they represent or toward foreign governments that allow their citizens to be abused. Some people have expressed shame and disgust at being part of the United States, which they see as responsible for the exploitation and repression of Third World peoples. Some may become depressed, experiencing deep-rooted feelings of hopelessness and powerlessness as they consider the immensity of the global factory and the seeming futility of struggles against it. Others find hope and inspiration as they witness the tenacity of people who continue to fight for justice against great odds.

Offering people time to express their feelings helps guide the discussion into the most fruitful channels by revealing what are the most important issues for the group. Allowing participants to voice their feelings can also help make the discussion more personal and meaningful for them, increasing their sense of involvement in the process. Asking others if they feel the same way can help bring people together.

Structure your discussion to promote full participation.

It is often necessary to think carefully about how to foster the fullest possible participation of everyone in a discussion. While people may still benefit from listening to a discussion in which only a few participate, many times those who are slowest to talk have the best insights to offer.

In groups that include both men and women, sexism is often a serious impediment to full participation. It is still very common for the men in a group to dominate a discussion, especially when questions of political analysis are concerned. Women have been particularly trained to believe that they cannot understand economics or other abstract matters.

MARTHA TABOR/IMPACT VISUALS

Numerous techniques have been developed to promote full participation in a meeting. On any given topic, you may wish to request brief reactions from everybody before opening up the discussion. Having someone call on speakers can prevent those who are more aggressive from monopolizing the floor. People who have not spoken previously can be called on in preference to those who have already had their say.

Another type of approach is to break the group up into smaller groups or pairs and ask people to spend five minutes discussing a particular question. Afterwards, they will return to the larger group with their minds and mouths already working.

Emphasize what is being done about the global factory.

To counteract feelings of helplessness about the global factory, it is important to talk about what is being done about it and what can be done about it, both in the United States and in other countries. Many campaigns are directed toward one or another specific aspect of the global factory, so that they are easier to grasp than the entire global system. Such activities may involve taking only small steps, but together they can add up to a major change.

Action campaigns in both the United States and the Third World are the focus of chapters 2 through 5 of the guide.

QUESTIONS FOR DISCUSSION

In this section, we offer sample questions on a variety of topics. You will probably want to pick and choose among them, depending on the type of activity you are planning. In a one-session program, for example, you might show a video and choose four or five questions to start the discussion off. In a more ongoing effort, these questions could help you to structure several different sessions.

Seeking Common Ground: The United States and the Third World

1. How do the lives of working people in the United States differ from those of workers in other countries such as Mexico or the Philippines? What are some of the differences in terms of wages? Living standards? Labor rights? Political rights? What about the militance and level of organization of workers' movements?

2. What do U.S. workers have in common with workers in Third World countries? What global developments affect both groups? Are they affected in the same way?

3. Are there some groups of workers in the U.S. whose living and working conditions are similar to those of workers in the Philippines or Mexico? What racial/ethnic groups do they belong to? What parts of the country do they live in? What industries do they work in? What kinds of jobs do they do?

4. Was there a time in U.S. history when most workers faced conditions similar to those in the Third World today? How and why did this change? What direction are things changing in today?

5. Do women workers face different problems than men: In the United States? In the Third World? Are the issues faced by women workers similar in different Third World countries? Between the United States and the Third World?

6. When U.S. garment and electronics firms move their production overseas, why do they hire mainly women? What are the effects of this trend on individual women? On their families and communities?

7. Why do workers in the Philippines and Mexico continue to organize, despite the threat of violence and plant closings?

8. How do labor rights and working conditions in Mexico and the Philippines affect working people in the United States?

9. How does the global factory affect different groups of working people in the United States (for example, industrial workers, service workers, professional and technical workers, small businesspeople, small farmers, farmworkers)?

10. Should U.S. working people be concerned about labor rights and working conditions in other countries? Why or why not?

Economics and Politics

1. What factors cause U.S. firms to move their production operations out of the country? What parts of the firm remain in the United States?

2. Who makes the decision to move jobs from the United States to a Third World country? What are they looking for in other countries? What are they trying to leave behind?

3. What do workers contribute to a factory? How are they affected when the plant closes? What should the firm's responsibility be to its workers?

4. What do communities contribute to a factory? How are they affected by plant closures? What should the firm's responsibility be to the community?

5. Think about terms like "Rustbelt" and "Sunbelt" in relation to U.S. industry. Where do you hear these terms? What assumptions do they imply?

Sunbelt newspapers on sale in Detroit, 1981.

6. Why are there such large wage differentials between the United States and Third World countries? Why are living standards in the United States higher? Are living standards here rising or falling: For you? For U.S. working people in general?

7. How would you feel about the United States if you were a Mexican worker in an assembly plant along the border?

8. Why do the governments of the Philippines and Mexico want to expand export production? Does export production help these countries to develop? What groups in these countries benefit from export-oriented development?

9. How does U.S. government economic policy support the export of jobs? Is there a difference between the policies of different administrations?

10. Who is helped by U.S. trade policy? Who is hurt? Are the needs and interests of working people taken into account in the debate over "protectionism" versus "free trade?" Why or why not?

11. How does U.S. foreign policy relate to the development of the global factory? What is the connection between U.S. economic involvement and military involvement: In the Philippines? In Mexico? Are corporate interests also at stake in war-torn areas like Central America or Angola?

12. In the United States, what do the federal and state governments do to help workers who lose their jobs as a result of the global factory? What should they do?

13. Who decides where and how U.S. wealth should be invested? Who should control investment decisions—inside the United States? For U.S. investments in other countries?

Moving Toward Action

1. What are the current tactics of the U.S. labor movement in dealing with the problem of the global factory? What seems the most promising about each of these approaches? What seems more problematic?

2. What other constituencies have a stake in challenging transnational corporations? What types of tactics are they adopting? What opportunities or obstacles do these approaches face?

3. What is the potential for broad coalition efforts in the United States around the global factory? What are some of the obstacles for different groups trying to build coalitions? What are some possible solutions to these obstacles?

4. How can people in the United States—workers and their unions and communities—try to stop or slow down plant closings? What are the difficulties they encounter in trying to influence companies that are moving jobs to other countries? Where we cannot stop plant closings, what can be done to lessen their harmful impact?

5. What would be the potential benefits of developing ties among workers and unions in different countries? How could this help people in the United States? What are the obstacles to developing such support? What is currently being done?

HOW LONG?
"How long can a company survive when we in America cannot buy its products? It can produce products at a huge profit today. But if I don't have a job, I can't buy that product. How long can this last?"

—Union activist, El Paso, Texas

PLANNING A LONGER PROJECT

The balance of this chapter offers specific suggestions for ways to structure a more focused, in-depth discussion. For some groups, these ideas may offer a way to plan several classes or study sessions. Others may see them as a point of departure for an ongoing research/action project.

We do not attempt to suggest what form such an ongoing project might take. Each group will face its own constellation of local problems and draw on its own combination of local energy and resources. Each will have its own angle on the global factory and why it has become a subject of interest.

Some existing approaches to activism are surveyed in chapter 5. The discussion below offers models of how some groups might begin exploring the problem.

Who Pays/Who Benefits?

Who benefits from the global factory and who pays the price? Ask your group to go through the costs and benefits of the global factory for different groups of people: U.S. corporations, the U.S. government, working people in the United States, workers in Third World countries, and economic elites and

governments of Third World countries. You might also want to look at the varying impact on different subgroups of the U.S. workforce, as in question 9 under "Seeking Common Ground" above.

Breaking down the analysis in this way helps to develop a sense of the conflicting interests at stake in the global factory. This approach offers a deeper understanding than the usual framework of considering benefits for the United States as a whole or for other countries as a whole.

After noting down people's initial responses so that everyone can see them, discuss each one. For example, does the global factory really offer lower prices to U.S. consumers or simply higher profits for transnational corporations? Do the jobs created in export-oriented industry really benefit workers in Third World countries?

After completing your analysis, you might ask again: Which group decided to organize things in this way? How might things be different if working people in the United States and the Third World had a role in making the policy decisions?

The Debate over Responsibility

To examine commonly held beliefs about the underlying causes of the development of the global factory, ask what groups are responsible for the movement of jobs to Third World countries. After noting the different answers, discuss why each group is perceived to be responsible and whether the belief is justified. How are these beliefs promoted? Who benefits from them?

The goal of this exercise is to help people recognize that the two groups most commonly held responsible for this trend—workers in the United States and Third World workers—are actually the groups that have the least control over the situation.

Another approach would be to confront directly stereotypes about U.S. and foreign workers. Ask people to list some common beliefs about the two groups and then ask where these stereotypes come from. How are they perpetuated? Who do they benefit?

As a parallel exercise, you might also want to examine ideas about different groups of U.S. workers: native-born and immigrant, documented and undocumented, unionized and nonunionized, men and women, younger and older. What about African-Americans, Latinos, whites, Asian-Americans, Native Americans? Why do members of these different subgroups tend to work in different types of jobs? Which subgroups are more jobs being created for, and why? Which subgroups are seeing their traditional sources of employment erode? For each of these groups, what stereotypes are you aware of that relate to work?

Examining Corporate Viewpoints

In the box on page 83, we have listed some statements made by corporate spokesmen interviewed in the film, *The Global Assembly Line*. Ask your group how they would respond to some of these remarks. If your group has seen the film, you might want to ask what they can remember the corporate representatives saying. Alternatively, you might simply present the quotes listed here.

Asking whether these statements are true can generate discussion on a range of themes related to the global factory. This technique can also arouse anger at the apparent callousness of the business spokesmen. Such anger offers an opportunity to discuss how the men shown are representatives of a system that makes them callous by treating people as mere factors of production and reducing human lives to labor costs.

The Debate over the *Maquiladoras*

When U.S. jobs are moved to Mexico, they generally end up as extremely low-paying jobs in the *maquiladoras*, or U.S.-owned assembly plants that line the Mexico-U.S. border. The U.S. Commerce Department views the *maquiladoras* as a positive way to increase U.S. "competitiveness." Debate over U.S. policy erupted in the major media in the fall of 1986, when the Commerce Department promoted a trade show in the Mexican resort town of Acapulco that was intended to encourage U.S. firms to set up *maquiladora* plants. In response to outcries from labor unions and members of Congress—who were outraged that public funds were being used to promote the export of U.S. jobs—the Commerce Department was forced to withdraw its sponsorship of the trade show. Promotion was turned over to a private firm, and "Expo *Maquila*" took place as planned in December 1986.

When the *New York Times* editorialized in support of the *maquiladora* program, both the International Union of Electronic Workers and AFSC responded with letters to the editor. Taken together, these three statements—reproduced on page 84—provide a good introduction to the debate over the costs and benefits of *maquilas*.

You may wish to distribute copies of these documents as an aid to discussion. Ask your group to identify the arguments for and against the *maquiladora* program. What additional arguments could be made on either side? What assumptions underlie these arguments? In what ways do these assumptions limit the possible responses?

The *maquila* program is explored in greater depth in chapter 3 on Mexico.

Research Project: Consumer Goods

Here and in the next section, we present ideas for more extended research projects. Chapter 7 lists some resources that explain how to carry out the types of research suggested.

For an illustration of the extent of the global assembly line, you might pose two questions:

- Where were the clothes you are wearing made?

- Where was your television made?

You can ask people to check the labels of their clothes or electronic items in their homes to see where these goods were made. Ask them to bring in lists of the different countries and locate the countries represented on a map of the world.

With competition from "cheap imports" receiving so much media attention, ask your group to consider in what sense their goods are imports. Were they made by U.S. companies manufacturing abroad, by foreign-owned manufacturers, or by the two in conjunction? If a label says "assembled in" a given country, it was probably made by a U.S. firm out of materials or components that were sent to that country from the United States under the "807 Program" (see chapter 1). If the label says "made in" a country, it may have been made by a foreign subsidiary of a U.S. firm, using materials purchased abroad; by a foreign corporation that was subcontracting for a U.S. firm, which then imported the materials into the United States; or by a foreign company that exports on its own to the United States. Your group might wish to research the ownership of the manufacturers listed on the labels.

Given the complexity of these international markets, how should we view media reports that speak only of "U.S. industry" and "foreign competition?" What realities are obscured by this terminology?

Some members of your group may be embarrassed that they buy clothes or other goods not made in the United States. An

QUALIFIED BY NATURE?

"The manual dexterity of the oriental female is famous the world over. Her hands are small and she works fast with extreme care. Who, therefore, could be better qualified by nature and inheritance to contribute to the efficiency of a bench-assembly production line than the oriental girl?"

—Malaysian promotional brochure, quoted in Of Common Cloth

Statements of Corporate Representatives

- For the U.S. to remain competitive, more and more lower-cost, lower-skilled jobs are going to—whether you like it or not—have to move offshore.

- They cannot find the American worker that wants to work on that job.

- It is in the political interest of the United States to transfer production work to countries like the Philippines and thereby stabilize the position of the United States in the Pacific Basin, or

in Africa, or in Latin America, wherever the process is to take place.

- You must find a home where labor is relatively peaceful and easy to manage.

- But these girls are all in their early years. They can take a lot of abuse. They abuse their bodies a lot.

- These jobs are going to provide a better degree of understanding of us Americans, of who we are and what we're all about.

Source: The Global Assembly Line

Hecho en Mexico

The maquila debate in the New York Times: The editorial at right was published January 5, 1987, in the wake of the controversy over Expo Maquila. The two letters below—one from the International Union of Electronic Workers and one from AFSC— appeared on January 26.

Does America's Government-sanctioned "maquiladora" program with Mexico keep American companies from moving operations to Asia? Or does it encourage American business to look for cheaper labor south of the border?

Either way, the program serves America's long-term interests: it reduces the cost of manufactured goods to consumers and shores up the faltering economy of a strategically important neighbor. Though pressure is building to limit the twin-plant maquiladoras or cut them back, Congress would be foolhardy to interfere.

Under twin-plant arrangements, Mexico allows American companies to bring in parts and production machinery, duty-free. Once the goods are assembled from the imported materials, Washington permits the companies to bring them back, paying tariffs only on the value added in Mexico.

As a result, some 250,000 Mexicans now work in a thousand American-owned plants clustered along the Rio Grande. Labor groups regard that as Government-sanctioned piracy of American jobs. But defenders of the program argue that if American companies aren't permitted to become cost-competitive by farming out low-skill, low-wage assembly work to Mexico, entire industries will be lost to,

say, Korea or Hong Kong. The supporters also point out that dollars spent in Mexico are far more likely to stimulate demand for American goods. The prosperity of many Texas border towns in fact depends on Mexican purchasing power.

Actually, much more is at stake than the unemployment rate in Detroit or El Paso. While individual workers may suffer in the short term, there is no evidence that trade destroys more jobs than it creates; the percentage of working-age Americans employed has never been higher.

Trade does, however, influence the sort of work Americans do, typically, in positive ways. Few people would happily make a career of the low-productivity jobs being exported to Juárez. Trade also affects what American wages can buy: imports drastically reduce the price of everything from cameras to clothes to cars.

The general argument for open trade is even more persuasive in the case of Mexico. Its economy is in crisis; ensuing political and economic strains are making Mexico a difficult neighbor. Maquiladora alone won't decisively change the future. But the prosperity that the program fosters along the border is one ray of hope. To darken it would be costly.

Letters

How U.S. and Mexican Workers Lose Together

To the Editor:

"Hecho en Mexico" (editorial, Jan. 5) exhibits a particularly misinformed view of the "maquiladora," or twin-plant, program, and its effect on the U.S. and Mexican economies.

You pose two questions: "Does America's Government-sanctioned 'maquiladora' program with Mexico keep American companies from moving operations to Asia? Or does it encourage American business to look for cheap labor south of the border?"

But in neither way are our interests served, not the interests of consumers, not the interests of workers and not the long-term interests of the United States economy.

No logical rationale is given as to why a job lost to Mexico is any better than one lost to South Korea or Hong Kong. Entire segments of the electrical and electronic industries, for example, have been lost to Mexico and elsewhere.

The $170 billion U.S. trade deficit has left unemployment rates at historically high levels — 1986 was the sixth straight year with unemployment rates in excess of 7 percent. Nor has the worker-consumer come out ahead in the cheap-import "bargain" — average real hourly earnings for U.S. production workers have declined over the last 15 years.

The day your editorial appeared, the A. O. Smith Corporation announced it was closing its motor plant in Union City, Ind., and moving the work to Mexico. Contrary to your view, these union members happily made their careers out of these jobs

and, like thousands of other American workers, would happily take them back.

U.S. plants are often just warehouses employing a few workers. Because all the production work is being done in Mexico, the program has brought few actual benefits to towns along the Mexican border. With wages averaging 50 cents an hour, it is hard to see how Mexican workers can afford to buy autos, appliances and other American-made goods.

The maquiladora program has not fostered prosperity for Mexican workers. Only American-based multinationals and a few Mexican elites have prospered under the scheme. U.S. tariff treatment of maquiladora products is aimed at squeezing every possible dollar out of the Mexican economy to pay off Mexico's international debt. Putting the Mexican economy through the "export development" wringer offers no ray of hope to Mexican or American workers.

How can you ignore the evidence presented last month before the House subcommittees chaired by John LaFalce and James Florio demonstrating the negative consequences of the program? American workers feel that it would be foolhardy for Congress not to restrict the use of maquiladoras by U.S. corporations.
WILLIAM H. BYWATER
President, International Union of Electronic Workers, A.F.L.-C.I.O.
Washington, Jan. 7, 1987

Subsidized Exploitation

To the Editor:

We at the American Friends Service Committee have been working along the Mexico-United States border for 30 years. That is why we can identify major issues that are not addressed in "Hecho en Mexico" ("Made in Mexico").

One central issue is the nature of the jobs being created. They are marginal, low-wage, dead-end jobs that exploit Mexican workers. The current average hourly wage rate in the maquiladoras is about 50 cents. This is 45 percent less than the rate in Hong Kong or Taiwan, two other countries to which U.S.-based corporations have moved their plants.

Maquiladora workers are almost exclusively young women 16 to 23 years old, many of whom are breadwinners for families consisting of parents, siblings and children. The wages do not sustain the workers and their families. Women workers in maquilas daily face deteriorating working conditions that include escalating production quotas, pressures and abuses from supervisors, and the dread and threat of being fired if they assert their rights under Mexico's labor laws or seek to improve their working conditions in any way.

Mexico lacks health and safety regulations. Dangerous levels of contamination exist in many maquiladoras. For example, the electronics industry depends heavily on the use of methylene chloride for cleaning components; recent research indicates

that this solvent is carcinogenic. Workers not only lack protective equipment when handling this liquid, but also many, unaware of its dangers, use it to wash their hands because it is an effective grease cutter.

A high percentage of workers suffer from arthritis, bronchitis, vision problems and serious respiratory diseases. Research is under way to investigate correlations between physically and mentally handicapped children and mothers who have worked in specific maquiladora industries.

Our experience with union members in the U.S. suggests they are increasingly aware of the impact of corporate practices on Mexican workers, as well as on themselves. The union movement is looking more closely at what kinds of industries are developed by the tax breaks afforded to U.S. parent corporations of maquiladoras. It is legitimate to question whether we should be subsidizing this kind of exploitation with our tax dollars.

In addition, the economies of the border are totally interrelated so that whatever occurs on one side affects the other. For instance, low wages on the Mexican side necessarily affect wages on this side, causing the Rio Grande Valley to have one of the lowest per capita incomes in the U.S. and one of the highest levels of unemployment.
ELIZABETH BAUMANN
Philadelphia, Jan. 8, 1987

alternative exercise would be to ask group members to visit different stores to see where clothing or electronic goods are manufactured. Ask your group to compare the prices of goods made in the United States with goods made in other countries. Be sure to have some people go to the most expensive stores in your community—they will find that some of the most costly garments are made in very low-wage countries.

Research Project: Local Involvement in the Global Economy

This project can be adapted to the situations of many types of groups, whether or not group members work directly for a transnational corporation.

With workplace groups, ask members of your group to think about how they might investigate their own employer. Are they part of a union they might turn to for information? If not, how might they use material from other unions, public libraries, or on-line services (see chapter 7) to ask questions without endangering themselves?

Here are some questions your group might want to explore: Does the company have any manufacturing facilities in other countries? Does it subcontract to foreign manufacturers? If the company does not currently have any manufacturing in other countries, do any of its competitors? What competitive pressures are placed on the company to also transfer production to countries where labor costs are lower? Are there labor-intensive parts of the existing production process that could be shipped to lower-wage countries?

This exercise can be done by many people in nonmanufacturing jobs also. Increasingly, data processing jobs in insurance, telecommunications, and banking are also moving to other countries.

If your group's members do not work in industry, or if they do not work for an industry that is threatened by the movement of jobs abroad, ask them to investigate how their community is affected by the global factory. People in the group may be indirectly affected by the actions of companies they do not work for, since entire communities suffer from the loss of jobs and the resulting loss of related employment, decline in the tax base, demand for social services, and social and personal costs.

Once group members identify the countries in which their companies (or major employers in their community) or their competitors are operating, ask them to

JIM WEST/IMPACT VISUALS

investigate the living and working conditions in those countries. What is the status of labor rights in the export processing zones in those countries? What rights do workers have outside the zones? What is U.S. foreign policy toward that country? If your group members belong to a union, does their international have any ties with workers or unions in that country? Does the AFL-CIO operate any of its international programs in that country?

Ask people to think about concrete possibilities for developing ties with workers or unions in the countries where their company operates—as individuals, through their local union, or through their international. Which type of cooperation would be most effective? What types of assistance could you and the workers in the other country give each other? How could you go about setting up this type of solidarity?

Even if people do not work for a company that might move to another country and there are no local companies that are likely to do so, ask them to think about how they are affected by the decline in wages and unionization that is a result of the global factory. Many companies that are not unionized may offer higher wages and provide better benefits in order to keep their employees from joining unions. In this and other ways the better conditions brought about by unionization have a general "spillover" effect on the conditions of all working people in the United States. What is happening to the nonunionized sector as unionized jobs are lost and labor unions lose power?

Detroit, 1987: A 16-year veteran of General Motors Clark Street Cadillac plant sits on the factory's steps the night before it was permanently closed.

**Labor Day parade,
New York City, 1988.**

Your group may also live in an area that is affected by the internal movement of jobs within the United States, not just the international aspects of the global factory. A little research into the history of your community can reveal a lot about the source of its contemporary problems. If you live in a traditionally industrial area in the Northeast or Midwest, how many industrial jobs have been lost in your community over the past ten years? The past twenty-five years? The past fifty years? How have average wages and the percentage of unionized jobs changed over that period? What about other social indicators such as poverty, unemployment, or infant mortality?

By contrast, if you live in an area of the country that industry is moving to, such as the Southwest, what changes has that caused in your community? How well do these jobs pay now in relation to what they formerly paid in older industrial areas? Are the jobs union or nonunion? What demands are placed on your community by industrial development (for example, increased need for social services, water resources, etc.)? Who pays for these "side effects" of development? Do plants come and stay, or do they come for a few years and then move on—perhaps to Mexico or another country?

7. Resources for Further Study/Action

AUDIOVISUALS

Most of the audiovisuals listed below are available for either sale or purchase in a variety of film and video formats. Contact the distributors for formats and costs.

Black Trade Unions in South Africa. Shows conditions of Black workers under apartheid, the pivotal role of Black unions in the anti-apartheid movement, and the support extended by U.S. unions. 23 minutes, 1986. AFL-CIO Educational Film Dept., 815 Sixteenth Street NW, Washington, DC 20006 (202/853-3000).

The Business of America. This film probes the assumption that corporate profit maximization will lead to economic well-being for U.S. working people. The film contrasts the traditional faith in free enterprise of two Pittsburgh steelworkers with the actual strategies of the former U.S. Steel Corporation. It considers alternative strategies for accountable economic decision-making, including worker ownership, targeted pension fund investment, and regional economic planning. 45 minutes, color, 1984. California Newsreel, 149 Ninth Street, No. 420, San Francisco, CA 94103 (tel. 415/621-6196; fax 415/621-6522).

Controlling Interest. Widely used film on transnational corporations and their impact on the world economy. With scenes from Brazil, Chile, Singapore, the Dominican Republic, and New England, shows the connections among economic concentration, the international movement of jobs, and the growth of militarism. 45 minutes, 1978. California Newsreel, 149 Ninth Street, No. 420, San Francisco, CA 94103 (tel. 415/621-6196; fax 415/621-6522).

Down and Out in America by Lee Grant. Interviews by Lee Grant with working people affected by farm foreclosures, the international movement of jobs, and homelessness. A vivid look at the human costs of U.S. economic policies. 60 minutes, 1986. Church World Service, PO Box 968, Elkhart, IN 46515 (219/264-3102).

Forget Not Our Sisters. Slide show on the impact of apartheid on Black women in South Africa and their role in the anti-apartheid movementt. Includes section on the role of U.S. corporations in supporting apartheid. 39 minutes, 1982. AFSC-Cambridge, 2161 Massachusetts Ave., Cambridge, MA 02140 (617/497-5273).

Girls Apart by C. Sheppard. Documentary portrait of two teenage South African girls, one Black, one a white Afrikaner. They take us into their homes and churches, introduce us to their families and communities, and share their hopes and fears. The girls never meet in the film and probably never will in real life. Moving depiction of the separate worlds dictated by apartheid. 40 minutes, 1988. California Newsreel, 149 Ninth Street, No. 420, San Francisco, CA 94103 (tel. 415/621-6196; fax 415/621-6522).

The Global Assembly Line by Lorraine Gray. Shows how women workers in Mexico, the Philippines, and the United States are affected by the international movement of jobs. Includes vivid scenes of strike actions in all three countries, as well as eye-opening statements by corporate spokesmen. 1 hour, 1983. New Day Films, 853 Broadway, Room 1210, New York, NY 10003 (212/477-4604).

Kababaihan: Filipina Portraits by Marie Boti and Malcolm Guy. A look at grassroots women activists in the Philippines involved in the years of organizing that ultimately toppled the Marcos regime. Also available in French. 40 minutes, video, 1989. Le Videographe, 4550 Garnier, Montreal, Quebec, Canada H2J 3S6 (514/521-2116).

Nosotros Trabajamos en la Costura (We Work in the Garment Trade). Slide show with audiocassette offering portraits of Puerto Rican women working in the garment industry in New York and offering historical background and context. 15 minutes, 1985. Puerto Rico Endowment, 1010 Vermont Ave., NW, Suite 801, Washington, DC 20005 (202/347-6859).

The People Will Not Be Silent by Dorie Krauss and Susie Sluyter. Video documentary of popular resistance in El Salvador; many interviews with labor activists. 30 minutes, 1988. Order from People Will Not Be Silent c/o 306 Summer Street, No. 3, Somerville, MA 02144 (617/628-5368).

Tiger by the Tale by Michal Goldman. Documents story of successful campaign by members of UAW Local 645 in Van Nuys, CA to prevent closure of GM plant. Scenes of workers' lives on the job and in the community, as well as community/labor coalition that emerged around this campaign. 40 minutes. Labor/Community Coalition to Keep GM Open, 6151 Van Nuys Blvd., Van Nuys, CA 91401 (213/931-9888).

Voices From a Steeltown by Tony Buba. Portrait of a

Access to Audiovisuals

The **Media Network** maintains an extensive database of films and videos on a broad range of themes that may be of interest to activists, teachers, or researchers. Also available are published guides to audiovisuals on selected themes such as environmental issues, Central America, and more. The group's quarterly newsletter, *MediaActive,* offers news and reviews of interest to media activists. For more information, contact the Media Network, 121 Fulton Street, New York, NY 10038 (212/619-3455).

declining industrial town in western Pennsylvania. The town's few remaining residents view their situation with a mix of stoicism, puzzlement, and humor as they reminisce about Braddock's heyday and try to figure out who is responsible for its slow death. 28 minutes, color, 1984. Braddock Chronicles, PO Box 426, Braddock, PA 15104 (412/351-4808).

We Didn't Want It to Happen This Way. Workers in Sioux City, Iowa, tell of the human costs of a decision by Zenith Corp. to move their jobs to Mexico and Taiwan. 30 minutes, 1979. AFL-CIO Educational Film Dept., 815 Sixteenth Street NW, Washington, DC 20006 (202/853-3000).

Who Killed Vincent Chin? by Chris Choy and Renee Tajima. Vincent Chin was a Chinese-American living in Detroit. He was beaten to death in 1982 by two men, one a foreman from an auto plant, who, believing he was Japanese, chose him as the target of their rage at massive layoffs in the auto industry. This film tells Chin's story and examines the racist violence and scapegoating of foreigners for U.S. economic problems that created the context for his murder. 60 minutes, 1986. Third World Newsreel, 335 W. 38th Street, New York, NY 10018 (212/947-9277).

A number of local plant closings groups have produced videos about their specific campaigns. Contact the Plant Closures Project in Oakland, CA for more information.

PAMPHLETS AND BRIEF PUBLICATIONS

Betrayal of Trust: Stories of Working North Carolinians. Recounts the struggle of workers at Schlage Lock described in chapter 5, along with other stories about the human casualties of state development policies. Available from Southerners for Economic Justice, PO Box 240, Durham, NC 27702 (919/683-1361).

Beyond Labour Issues: Women Workers in Asia. Report based on Asian regional conference exploring new organizing strategies to meet the needs of women workers, especially in the TNC workforce. 1988, Committee for Asian Women; U.S. distribution by Women's International Resource Exchange, 475 Riverside Drive, Room 570, New York, NY 10115.

Early Warning Manual Against Plant Closings by the Midwest Center for Labor Research. Suggestions and case studies of successful early warning campaigns. Revised edition, 1988; also available in Spanish. Related training programs and technical assistance also available. $15 plus $1.50 postage to unions and community groups; $25/$50 others from MCLR, 3411 W. Diversey, No. 10, Chicago, IL 60647 (312/278-5418).

From Bonding Wires to Banding Women. Pamphlet based on the 1986 microtechnology consultation in the Philippines described in chapter 5. Published in 1988 by the Center for Women's Resources, 43 Roces Avenue, Quezon City, The Philippines. Distribution outside Asia by Participatory Research Group, 394 Euclid Avenue, Room 308, Toronto, Ontario M6G 2S9, Canada.

Maquiladoras and Toxics: The Hidden Costs of Production South of the Border by Leslie Kochan. Explores toxic threat to both Mexican and U.S. workers caused by proliferation of *maquila* plants. AFL-CIO Publication 186, 1989.

Meeting the Corporate Challenge: A Handbook on Corporate Campaigns. Discussion of contemporary strategies of transnational corporations and case studies of community/labor responses internationally. Published 1985 by the Transnationals Information Exchange, Paulus Potterstraat 20, 1071 DA Amsterdam, The Netherlands (tel. 020 766 724).

Minangkabau: Stories of People Versus TNCs in Asia. Case histories and strategies in industry and agribusiness. 1981; available from Urban-Rural Mission, Christian Conference of Asia, 57 Peking Road, 5/F, Kowloon, Hong Kong.

Partners or Predators? International Trade Unionism and Asia. An introduction to international trade union structures, their origins and politics, and the major debates that involve the international union movement today. Published as part of continuing series, *Asia Labour Monitor.* 1989; Asia Monitor Resource Center, 444 Nathan Rd., 8-B, Kowloon, Hong Kong.

Plant Closures: Myths, Realities, Responses by Gilda Haas and the Plant Closures Project. Discusses the reasons for plant closures and surveys the worker and community movement against them. 1985; $4.75 from South End Press, 116 St. Botolph Street, Boston, MA 02115.

Real World Macro: A Macroeconomics Reader from Dollars & Sense. Easy-to-understand explanation of current trends in U.S. economy, discussing unemployment, inflation, affirmative action and equality, the new service economy, fiscal and monetary policy, and more. Updated 1988; available from Economic Affairs Bureau, One Summer Street, Somerville, MA 02143.

Short Circuit: Women on the Global Assembly Line and **Short Circuit: Women in the Automated Office.** Two separate pamphlets, one on women's labor in electronics production and the other on the effect of new information technology on women's work. $3 each from Participatory Research Group, 394 Euclid Avenue, Room 308, Toronto, Ontario M6G 2S9, Canada.

The Struggle to Save Morse Cutting Tool: A Successful Community Campaign by Barbara Doherty. A complete account of the United Electrical Workers campaign to save a machine tool plant from closure. 1986; $2 from Labor Education Center, Southeastern Massachusetts University, North Dartmouth, MA 12747.

Taking on General Motors: A Case Study of the UAW Campaign to Keep GM Van Nuys Open by Eric Mann. Fascinating, detailed account of successful effort by autoworkers to prevent a shutdown by using the threat of a boycott of GM products. 1987; $20 from Institute of Industrial Relations, UCLA, Los Angeles, CA 90024.

Tales of the Filipino Working Women. Personal testimonies collected by the Committee for Asian Women. 1984; US$ 2.50 from Committee for Asian Women, 57 Peking Road, 4/F, Kowloon, Hong Kong (tel. 3-72 6150).

Trade's Hidden Costs: Worker Rights in a Changing World Economy. Publication of the International Labor Rights Working Group profiled in chapter 5. 1988; $3.95 from

Institute for Policy Studies, 1601 Connecticut Avenue, NW, Washington, DC 20009.

Tunnel Vision: Labor, the World Economy, and Central America by Daniel Cantor and Juliet Schor. Background on the debate within the labor movement over U.S. intervention in Central America; sponsored by Policy Alternatives for the Caribbean and Central America. 1987; $5 from South End Press, 116 St. Botolph Street, Boston, MA 02115.

Women in the Global Factory by Annette Fuentes and Barbara Ehrenreich. Pioneering work on how women's labor is exploited by TNCs in the United States and the Third World. 1983; $3.75 from South End Press, 116 St. Botolph Street, Boston, MA 02115.

Women Working Worldwide: The International Division of Labor in the Electronics, Clothing and Textile Industries. Articles based on 1983 international conference. US$ 1.75 from War on Want, 467 Caledonian Road, London N7, UK.

BOOKS FOR IN-DEPTH STUDY

Bitter Choices: Blue Collar Women in and out of Work by Ellen Israel Rosen. Report on study of women assembly workers in New England. Although limited to married women, the book provides a useful partial portrait of women workers in declining industries. 219 pages. Chicago: University of Chicago Press, 1987.

Daughters in Industry: Work Skills and Consciousness of Women Workers in Asia, Noeleen Heyzer, Ed. Articles from ten Asian countries on industrialization, high-technology industry, and women workers' movements. 395 pages. Kuala Lumpur, Malaysia: Asian and Pacific Development Center, 1988. Available from APDC, Persiaran Duta, PO Box 12224, Kuala Lumpur, Malaysia.

The Deindustrialization of America: Plant Closings, Community Abandonment, and the Dismantling of Basic Industry by Barry Bluestone and Bennett Harrison. Comprehensive study of the erosion of the U.S. manufacturing base and its effects on local communities and the national economy. 323 pages, $8.95. New York: Basic Books, 1982.

Distant Neighbors by Alan Riding. In-depth analysis of how Mexico and the United States view each other which attempts to uncover the roots of misunderstandings and misinterpretations. New York: Alfred Knopf, 1985.

Export Processing Free Zones in Developing Countries: Implications for Trade and Industrialization Policies, UN Conference on Trade and Development. New York: United Nations, 1985.

For We Are Sold, I and My People: Women and Industry on Mexico's Frontier by Maria Patricia Fernandez Kelly. Classic study of the *maquiladora* industry and its effects on Mexican women. 217 pages; $14.95. Albany, NY: State University of New York Press, 1983.

From Tank Town to High Tech: The Clash of Community and Industrial Cycles by June Nash. Study of high-tech industry that explores the interconnections among militarization, the restructuring of U.S. economy, and the impact of these trends on individual, family, and community life.

368 pages; $18.95. Albany, NY: State University of New York Press, 1989.

The Great U-Turn: Corporate Restructuring and the Polarization of America by Bennett Harrison and Barry Bluestone. Six years after *The Deindustrialization of America* the same authors explore the current impact of corporate mergers and the global factory on the U.S. economy. 242 pages; $19.95. New York: Basic Books, 1988.

Industrial Women Workers in Asia, copublished by the Committee for Asian Women and Isis International. Articles from throughout the region on TNCs, working conditions, and organizing strategies. Rome: Isis International, 1985. See listing for Isis International under "Aids to Research" for contact information.

Modern Mexico: State, Economy and Social Conflict, Nora Hamilton & Timothy Harding, Eds., Latin American Perspectives Reader, Vol. 1, 1986. San Mateo, CA: Sage Publications, 1986.

Of Common Cloth: Women in the Global Textile Industry, Wendy Chapkis and Cynthia Enloe, Eds. Articles from Europe, Asia, and the United States on the international division of labor in textiles, homeworking, workers' movements and strategies, and more. Based on 1982 international conference. Amsterdam: Transnational Institute, 1983. Available from TNI, Paulus Potterstraat 20, 1071 DA Amsterdam, The Netherlands.

Patriarchy and Accumulation on a World Scale: Women in the International Division of Labour by Maria Mies. London: Zed Books, 1986.

Race, Gender, and Work: A Multicultural Economic History of Women in the United States by Teresa Ammot and Julie Matthei. Explores the distinct economic histories of African-American, American Indian, Chicana, Chinese, Euro-American, Filipina, Japanese, and Puerto Rican women, detailing the complex hierarchy of race, class, and gender in the U.S. workforce. Includes historical analysis, women's testimony, and accounts of collective action.

Boston: South End Press, forthcoming (January 1990).

Technology and Structural Unemployment: Reemploying Displaced Adults, Office of Technology Assessment, U.S. Congress. A comprehensive government report that includes an excellent chapter on displaced workers. 1986; free from OTA, Washington, DC 20510.

Transnational Corporations and Labor: A Directory of Resources, Thomas Fenton and Mary Heffron, Eds. New guide from Third World Resources (see listing below under "Aids to Research." Listings include publications, audio-visuals, and organizations. Maryknoll, NY: Orbis Books, 1989.

Trilateralism: The Trilateral Commission and Elite Planning for World Management, Holly Sklar, Ed. Explanation of how the U.S., European, and Japanese governments work together with transnational corporations to manage economic and political developments on a global level. 604 pages, $8. Boston: South End Press, 1980.

Women, Men, and the International Division of Labor, June Nash and Maria Patricia Fernandez Kelly, Eds. International collection of articles exploring different facets of the global factory, workers' movements, and women's survival strategies. Albany, NY: State University of New York Press, 1982.

Work Transformed: Automation and Labor in the Computer Age by Harvey Shaiken. See especially the section on "The Global Factory," pp. 234-246. Lexington, MA: Lexington Books, 1984.

PERIODICALS

The publications listed below frequently report on concerns related to the themes of this guide. In addition many of the groups listed in the section on organizations publish newsletters about their specific area of interest.

Asian Women Workers Newsletter, quarterly bulletin of Committee for Asian Women. Regional focus and frequent reports on struggles involving transnational corporations. Subscriptions $4 from CAW, 57 Peking Road, 4/F, Kowloon, Hong Kong (tel. 3-72 6150).

Dollars & Sense, monthly review of economics in the United States and internationally from a socialist perspective; written in popular language and assumes little prior knowledge of economics. Subscriptions $19.50 from Economic Affairs Bureau, One Summer Street, Somerville, MA 02143 (617/628-8411).

Global Electronics, monthly bulletin on trends in the electronics industry. U.S. subscriptions $12 from Pacific Studies Center, 222C View Street, Mountain View, CA 94041 (415/969-1545). See also listing under "Aids to Research" below.

International Labour Reports, bimonthly review of international news and trends. Subscriptions 10 pounds individuals, 20 pounds institutions from ILR/Mayday Publications, 2/4 Oxford Road, Manchester, UK M1 5QA. U.S. contact: Kim Scipes, PO Box 5036, Berkeley, CA 94705.

Labor Notes, monthly news bulletin on labor movement developments in the U.S. and internationally. Subscriptions $10 individuals, $20 institutions from Labor Education and Research Project, 7435 Michigan Avenue, Detroit, MI 48210 (313/842-6262).

Labor Research Review, forum for community and labor activists addressed to a wider labor audience. Theme issues include plant closings movement, women and labor, international labor solidarity, and more. Published twice a year. Subscriptions $13, $20 for libraries from Midwest Center for Labor Research, 3411 W. Diversey, Chicago, IL 60647 (312/278-5418).

The Other Side of Mexico, news, interviews, and analysis from Mexico's popular movements. Published six times a year in English and Spanish. Subscriptions $10 to individuals, $18 to institutions in Latin America; $15 and $20 in North America and Europe. Order from Equipo Pueblo, A.P. 27-467, 06760 Mexico, D.F.; subscription checks payable to Carlos A. Heredia/Equipo Pueblo.

Wiser Links, international journal on women's issues with frequent reports on labor issues. Subscriptions 3 to 12 pounds on sliding scale from Women's International Resource Centre, 173 Archway Road, London N6 5BL, UK (tel: 341-4403).

Women in Action, quarterly journal of Isis International. News, reviews, action alerts from global women's movement, with emphasis on Third World countries. Published in English and Spanish. Subscriptions $20 to individuals and women's groups, $30 institutions. See addresses in listing under "Aids to Research" below.

Workers' Advocate, bimonthly publication on developments in the progressive Philippine labor movement. Available from Ateneo Center for Social Policy and Public Affairs, Room 230, Faura Hall, PO Box 154, 1099 Manila, The Philippines.

AIDS TO RESEARCH

The DataCenter. Indispensable information source on transnational corporations from a critical perspective. Offers computerized search service with files on more than 6000 corporations and 400 subject areas in politics and economics. Also available is a clipping service covering 350 publications. Regular publications include *Plant Shutdowns Monitor* and *Corporate Responsibility Monitor*. 464 19th Street, Oakland, CA 94612 (415/835-4692).

IBON Databank. Center for alternative information on the Philippine economy. Publishes monthly bulletin and special directories, including the *Directory of TNCs in the*

Philippines (1988). Room 303, SCC Building, 3892 Magsaysay Road, Sta. Mesa, Metro Manila, The Philippines.

Isis International. Women's international information and communication service with emphasis on Third World women's movements. Maintains two computerized documentation centers with databases on audiovisuals, women's publications, women's organizations, and more. Publications include quarterly bulletin *Women in Action* (see periodicals listing above) and semi-annual book series. Includes frequent reports on labor issues and transnational corporations. All materials issued in English and Spanish. Spanish-language resource center: Isis Internacional, Casilla 2067, Correo Central, Santiago, Chile (tel. 490 271). English-language center, formerly in Rome, will be moving to Asia in early 1990. U.S. contact: Isis International, PO Box 25711, Philadelphia, PA 19144.

Center for Popular Economics. Training courses and publications to make economic information accessible to grassroots community activists. PO Box 785, Amherst, MA 01004 (413/545-0743).

Center for U.S.-Mexican Studies. Research in social science and history, graduate and undergraduate student training, publications, and public service activities. Recent publications include *Maquiladoras: Annotated Bibliography and Research Guide, 1980-1988,* a book-length guide. University of California-San Diego, D-010, La Jolla, CA 92093.

Pacific Studies Center. Publisher of *Global Electronics* (see listing under "Periodicals" above.) Also coordinates Global Electronics Information Project, a network of activists, researchers, and journalists. File searches are also available on specific topics at flexible rates. 222C View Street, Mountain View, CA 94041 (415/969-1545).

Third World Resources. Publishes quarterly review of resources from and about the Third World, including publications, audiovisuals, and organizations. Also publishes book-length resource guides on specific topics; see listing for *Transnational Corporations and Labor* under "Books for In-Depth Study" above. Previous resource guides include *Women in the Third World; Food, Hunger, Agribusiness;* and several regional directories. Affiliated with the DataCenter. 464 19th Street, Oakland, CA 94612 (415/835-4692).

UN Center on Transnational Corporations. Research and policy analysis center with strong focus on TNCs and environmental issues in the Third World. Numerous publications detailing TNC activities. 2 UN Plaza, New York, NY 10017 (212/963-6764).

Women's International Resource Exchange. Translates and publishes wide variety of materials from women's movements in Third World countries, with many items on global corporations. Also distributes some Third World publications. 475 Riverside Drive, Room 570, New York, NY 10115.

The following mainstream resources are also useful for investigating particular companies' and may be found in most business libraries:

The Directory of American Firms Operating Overseas.

The International Directory of Corporate Affiliations—Lists divisions and subsidiaries of firms around the world.

Predicasts F&S Index International—Indexes international news coverage by company name and industry.

InfoTrack—This computer system, available in some libraries, will search over 1000 periodicals for coverage of a given company.

ORGANIZATIONS

Contact information is provided below for groups whose work is described in this guide. Other useful resource organizations are listed above under "Aids to Research."

Alliance for Philippine Concerns, PO Box 170219, San Francisco, CA 94117 (415/540-5230)

Asian Immigrant Women Advocates, 310 8th Street, No. 205, Oakland, CA 94607 (415/268-0192)

Comité de Apoyo, PO Box 1206, Edinburg, TX 78539

Congress of South African Trade Unions (COSATU), PO

American Friends Service Committee

Two AFSC programs collaborated to produce *The Global Factory:* the **Maquiladora Project** and the **Women and Global Corporations Project**. Both may be contacted through AFSC's National Office, 1501 Cherry Street, Philadelphia, PA 19102.

The **Maquiladora Project** (tel. 215/241-7129) is part of AFSC's Mexico-U.S. Border Program. Its concern is to increase public awareness of the negative impacts of *maquiladoras* on workers in both Mexico and the United States. It works with binational organizations at the border in support of women workers in the *maquiladoras*. On a national level, it shares information about *maquiladora* issues with journalists, public officials, and other organizations and activists.

The **Women and Global Corporations Project** (tel. 215/241-7181) is part of AFSC's Nationwide Women's Program (NWP). This project works to share information with activists and researchers on how working and living conditions for women and their communities are affected by transnational corporations, and how women around the world are organizing in response. Efforts focus on six key transnational industries: electronics, textiles, pharmaceuticals, tourism/prostitution, media, and agribusiness.

The project issues a quarterly bulletin as the center section of NWP's publication, *Listen Real Loud: News of Women's Liberation Worldwide*. It also maintains a small resource center and speakers network, and collaborates with grassroots organizations and other AFSC programs on specific projects.

Box 1019, Johannesburg 2000, South Africa (tel: 27 11 492 1440)

CRUCUL, c/o Norm Harper, UAW Local 2100, 2500 Main Street, Buffalo, NY 14212 (716/837-5110)

Federation for Industrial Retention and Renewal, 3411 W. Diversey, Chicago, IL 60647 (312/278-5418)

GABRIELA, PO Box 4386, Manila 2800, The Philippines

GABRIELA Support Network (U.S.), P.O. Box 343, New York, NY 10018 (212/629-0849)

Highlander Center, Rte. 3, Box 370, New Market, TN 37820 (615/933-3443)

Hometowns Against Shutdowns, 48 Kentwood Blvd., Bricktown, NJ 08723 (201/840-1723)

Interfaith Center for Corporate Responsibility, 475 Riverside Drive, New York, NY 10115 (212/870-2623)

Interfaith Economic Crisis Organizing Network, 475 Riverside Drive, New York, NY 10115 (212/870-3832)

Institute for Policy Studies, 1601 Connecticut Avenue NW, Washington, DC 20009 (202/234-9382)

International Labor Rights Working Group, Box 68, 110 Maryland Avenue, SE, Washington, DC 20002 (202/546-4304)

Kilusang Mayo Uno (May First Movement), Third Floor, Jopson Building, 510 M. Earnshaw Street, Sampaloc, Manila, The Philippines

Labor Committee Against Apartheid (New York), c/o ACTWU, 15 Union Square West, New York, NY 10003

Midwest Center for Labor Research, 3411 W. Diversey, Chicago, IL 60647 (312/278-5418)

La Mujer Obrera, 1113 East Yandell, El Paso, TX 79902 (915/533-9710)

Office Technology Education Project, c/o Lisa Gallatin, 6 Newsome Park, Jamaica Plain, MA 02130 (617/738-5447)

Philippine Workers Support Committee, PO Box 11208, Moilili Station, Honolulu, HI 96828 (808/595-7362)

Plant Closures Project, 433 Jefferson, Oakland, CA 94607 (415/834-5656)

Santa Clara Center for Occupational Safety and Health, 760 N. First Street, San Jose, CA 95112 (408/9998-4050)

Connecting with Mexico

Even though the desire for people-to-people communication across the Mexico-U.S. border is great, relatively few print and audiovisual resources were identified for inclusion in this guide. Those wishing to communicate directly with grassroots movements in Mexico may want to contact one of the organizations listed below.

Mexico-U.S. Dialogos Program, 51 8th Avenue, Brooklyn, NY 11217 (718/230-3628)—Facilitates binational grassroots dialog through research, policy analysis, and public education.

Mujer a Mujer/Woman to Woman, A.P. 24-553, Col. Roma, 06700 Mexico, D.F.; or PO Box 12322, San Antonio, TX 78212 (512/735-2629)--Binational women's group based in Mexico City that organizes exchange visits between grassroots women's groups in Mexico and the United States. Publishes *Correspondencia,* a quarterly bulletin on women in Mexico's popular movements.

SEDEPAC (Servicio, Desarrollo, y Paz, AC; Service, Development, and Peace), Huatusco 39, Col. Roma Sur, 06760 Mexico, D.F. (tel. 905 584 1578)—Peace and justice organization that supports grassroots movements in Mexico. The Women's Program sponsors a Maquila Project that is tied into a national network of researchers and activists.

Southerners for Economic Justice, PO Box 240, Durham, NC 27702 (919/683-1361)

Transnationals Information Exchange, Paulus Potterstraat 20, 1071 DA Amsterdam, The Netherlands (tel. 020 766 724)

Tri-State Conference on Steel, 300 Saline Street, Pittsburgh, PA 15207 (412/421-1980)

UNTS (National Union of Salvadoran Workers), 1300 Connecticut Avenue NW, Room 808, Washington, DC 20036 (202/ 857-52445)

U.S./Guatemala Labor Education Project, c/o District 65/UAW, 13 Astor Place, 7th Floor, New York, NY 10003

Glossary

colonialism   The economic and political system of colonialism dates back to the early 1500s, when western European countries like England, France, and Spain began to conquer and rule as their colonies virtually all of Asia, Africa, and Latin America. Other countries, like the United States, were also settled as European colonies. The wealth removed from these colonies and the slave labor of their people paid for the industrial development of Europe and North America. Although the era of colonialism ended after World War II, its legacy persists. The former colonies are the poor nations of the world today, and their former rulers are still the world's richest nations.

capital-intensive   Refers to industrial processes in which machinery or capital goods account for a relatively high percentage of the total costs of production. Compare *labor-intensive*.

conglomerate   A large corporation composed of many unrelated businesses joined in a single corporate entity. Most TNCs are conglomerates.

currency devaluation   *Currency* is the form of money in use in a particular country. For example, Mexico's currency is the peso; the U.S. currency is the dollar. When a currency is devalued, its value declines relative to other currencies. Before 1982, one U.S. dollar could be purchased for 25 Mexican pesos. In one year, the peso was devalued so that a dollar cost 150 pesos. By 1988 a dollar cost 2300 pesos.

deindustrialization   This is a new word, coined in the 1970s to refer to the movement of industrial jobs out of the United States. Compare *reindustrialization*.

deskilling   This word was coined to refer to the reorganization of work processes to require less skill and training on the part of workers. Such reorganization is usually accomplished through automation and breaking down complex jobs into different steps performed by different workers. Deskilling reduces the bargaining power of workers because they can be more easily replaced.

disinvestment   The withdrawal of capital investment from an enterprise or industry. Disinvestment may take many forms, such as shutting down a plant, selling off some of a firm's subsidiaries, or failing to make continuing investments in upkeep and modernization.

dislocated worker   Someone who has lost a job because of plant closures or layoffs in a particular company or industry.

duty   See *tariff*.

eminent domain   The power of government to condemn and take possession of private property for "public purposes." This power has traditionally been used to acquire property for highways and other such projects. Today, some local governments are exploring the use of eminent domain for the prevention of plant shutdowns, as described in chapter 2.

export processing zones (EPZs)   Special areas created by some Third World governments to attract foreign investment in industry. Corporations operating in these zones typically import components for assembly in their factories in the EPZs. The finished or semi-finished goods are then exported to the United States or another foreign market. EPZ regulations generally include tax breaks for TNCs and a weakening of environmental restrictions and labor rights.

foreign exchange   The amount of foreign currency available to a government for purchasing goods or services from other countries. For example, when a U.S.-based corporation invests dollars in the economy of a country like Mexico, these dollars are then available for buying imports or making interest payments on Mexico's debt to U.S. banks.

free trade zones   See *export processing zones*.

gender   In our usage, a person's *sex* refers to their biological identity as female or male. *Gender* refers to all those aspects of femaleness or maleness that are mainly produced by history and culture, rather than biology. For example, electronics assembly workers are usually women because the workforce is divided by gender—there is no biological or "natural" reason why women are hired to do this work.

homeworking   Assembly work that is subcontracted by an employer to individual workers, usually women, who work in their homes and are generally paid by the piece. Homework usually pays sub-minimum wages and often leads to unsafe working conditions and child labor. In the United States, a ban on homework dating back more than forty years was lifted by the Reagan Administration.

informal sector   That part of the economy that operates outside any stable structure of agreements between employer and employee or regulation by the state. Examples include street vendors; homeworking (see); work performed "off the books"; and the underground economy of drugs, prostitution, and other illegal enterprises. Workers in the informal sector seldom pay taxes and are almost never protected by minimum wage requirements or other labor laws. A worldwide growth in the informal sector is a central feature of the contemporary global economy.

labor-intensive   Refers to industrial processes in which labor costs make up a relatively high percentage of the total costs of production, as opposed to *capital-intensive* (see).

maquiladoras   Spanish word for foreign-owned plants that operate in Mexico, using local labor to assemble goods for the U.S. and other foreign markets. The policies of both the U.S. and Mexican governments encourage U.S. businesses to transfer jobs to Mexican subsidiaries or subcontractors. *Maquilas*, as they are also known, are a type of export processing plant (see *export processing zone*). They are also often known as *twin plants* (see).

nationalization   The process by which a government restores national control of corporations or industries that are owned by foreign TNCs—usually by buying out the foreign corporations; occasionally by seizing their assets. This term is also used when ownership of a certain industry is transferred from the private sector to the government within a particular country.

productivity   A measure of how many goods or services can be produced by individual workers. For example, with better equipment workers can produce more for the same amount of effort—their productivity has been increased. Speed-ups are also an attempt to increase productivity by forcing workers to intensify their efforts.

reindustrialization   The reintroduction of industry into areas that have lost industrial employment. Compare *deindustrialization*.

subsidiary   A corporation that is owned by another, larger corporation. Transnational corporations have subsidiaries in many different countries, which operate in part as separate enterprises but are centrally owned and controlled.

subsistence agriculture   Agriculture in which crops are grown for the immediate use of a family or community, rather than for sale.

tariff   A tax charged on goods that move across international borders.

Third World   The term *Third World* refers to the nations of Africa, Asia, and Latin America. These nations are the former colonies of western Europe and the United States (see *colonialism*). We prefer the term Third World to "developing" or "underdeveloped" countries because it highlights the history of unequal relationships among groups of nations over the past 500 years.

Originally, the "first world" referred to the advanced capitalist nations (North America, western Europe, and Japan) and the "second world" was the socialist countries. Today, however, these terms are seldom used.

transnational corporation (TNC)   A corporation that operates in more than one country. In the post-World War II era, TNCs have come to dominate the global economy, and some large TNCs are richer and more powerful than many national governments.

twin plants   Another name for *maquiladoras* (see). In the border economy, a U.S.-owned plant on the Mexican side is frequently paired with a "twin" on the U.S. side owned by the same company. Although both twins supposedly generate substantial employment, in fact the U.S. twins seldom employ many people and often function mainly as warehouses.